SPIRITUAL
EMPOWERMENT

ALBERT C. GAW, M.D.

Published in the United States of America

Brilliant Books Literary
137 Forest Park Lane Thomasville
North Carolina 27360 USA

ISBN
Paperback: 979-8-88945-213-3
E-book: 979-8-88945-214-0
Hardback: 979-8-88945-215-7

The author, a psychoanalytically trained psychiatrist and Christian believer, has obviously studied his subject in depth and thought deeply about the relationship between psychological and spiritual aspects of the human person. He offers those of his own tradition as a way of understanding the meaning of the Scriptures and how it can be applied to their lives. His book should also be of considerable interest to those who seek a broader understanding of those with a different perspective and religious tradition.

Sara Charles, M.D.
Professor of Psychiatry (Emerita)
University of Illinois School of Medicine at Chicago

Albert Gaw has succeeded in writing an insightful, creative, and integrative account of Daniel from the Old Testament. He brings to bear the mind of a trained and wise psychiatrist who deeply understands the Scripture and biblical teachings. By integrating the knowledge of the fields of psychiatry and psychology, as well as his own experiences, he draws out lessons learned from Daniel's dreams and prophetic visions. These lessons deal with Christianity, spirituality, and earthly life. Dr. Gaw succeeds in providing a refreshing and inspiring account of major issues, such as the existence of suffering, evil, redemption, and the riches of faith and persistence.

Dr. Gaw's analysis and interpretations of Daniel constitute a major contribution. In addition, his final chapters bring home a message of empowerment, hope, inspiration, and triumph. The lessons from understanding Daniel within the context of psychiatry allow Dr. Gaw to draw implications for how to proactively deal with adversity, illness, and pain as well as to promote love and positive growth.

Thus the book touches on the spiritual, intellectual, professional, and applied-practical aspects of life.

Stanley Sue, Ph.D.
Professor of Psychology and Director, Center for Excellence in Diversity
Palo Alto University
Palo Alto, California

EMPOWERED focuses on Daniel as an example of faith and other practical virtues, which can be helpfully understood in light of both modern psychiatry and the rest of Scripture. Students of both will appreciate Dr. Gaw's emphasis on ways for believers to pursue the critically important goal of living more integrated lives.

John Peteet, M.D.
Associate Professor of Psychiatry
Harvard Medical School

Albert Gaw's "Empowered" is a wonderful exploration of the Book of Daniel and an exposition as to how a deeper understanding of Scripture can positively impact one's life.

"Empowered" begins with what Dr. Gaw defines as the "objective manifestation" of Daniel's psychospirituality, encompassing Daniel's encounters with the Babylonian and Persian kings. Then there is a section on Daniel's dreams and prophetic visions identified by Dr. Gaw as Daniel's "subjective manifestations" of his psychospirituality. "Empowered" also includes a very thoughtful and helpful section on 10 ways that psychospirituality can empower the life of the reader.

Gaw's deep faith and extensive clinical skills as a renowned psychiatrist shine thru throughout this work. It is a book to be read, re-read and studied. It will enrich people of faith and all who seek a deeper understanding of psychospirituality and empowerment.

John S. McIntyre, M.D.
Clinical Professor of Psychiatry, University of Rochester
Past-President, American Psychiatric Association

CONTENTS

PART 3
10 Lessons to Empower Your Life

DEDICATION

Tina.

My Mom, Tio Kong Piak (Chao H. Huang), who left us too soon.

My teachers and spiritual mentors, the late Rev. Joseph and Marion Esther, Tena Holkeboer, and Encarnacion Go Beltran. Though they have rested, they still speak.

FOREWORD

Empowered by Albert C. Gaw, M.D. demonstrates the powerful use of a unique combination of two perspectives (a psycho-spiritual approach) from which to understand a short but significant portion of the Bible that is rich in both history and symbolism. Rather than just "psychologize" Scripture, Dr. Gaw blends psychology and spirituality. Dr. Gaw sees "spirituality" as a relating of the heavenly and the earthly and that incarnational spirituality is at the heart of understanding spirituality in the Christian sense as opposed to some religions that see spirituality as related to the "otherworldly." This approach gives both the professional and the lay reader a workable tool for understanding and using the Book of Daniel.

The book is divided into three parts: Daniel's Encounters with the Babylonian and Persian Kings, His Dream and Visions, and Ten Practical Applications. It covers the theoretical and practical, ancient literature and modern scientific findings.

Equally important, Dr. Gaw provides the reader with a most helpful appendix that focuses on methodological and conceptual issues. His charts and his breakdowns of various parts of the book are wonderfully helpful tools for both the reader and the teacher. The book does more than just give answers; it gives tools that will allow the reader to develop his or her own answers.

Dr. Gaw writes clearly and insightfully. Ever since the pioneering days of Harry Emerson Fosdick -- the most noted Protestant radio preacher of the Riverside Church and the radio program National Vespers of the 1930, scholars and the public have come to see the validity of relating psychological insights to biblical narratives. The fact that the Bible is a reflection on human experience as well as spiritual learning has been well established. Many of those studies however, have been by students of religion who apply what they have learned from psychology and psychotherapy. Dr. Gaw as a man of the psychological world itself brings that background to the same studies. As such, this new book is what academics call a true "contribution to knowledge."

I personally appreciate this work and commend it for those who would like to understand Daniel for themselves and open up Daniel for other people. When I was in my early theological studies, our professors suggested that we not preach on Daniel or the Book of Revelation until we had had five to ten years of work in bible study for our own preaching. Had those professors had this book, I am sure that they would have said simply, "Do not preach on Daniel until you have made use not only of Dr. Gaw's insights but also his methodology."

Rev. James G. Emerson, BD and PhD
Pastor Emeritus, Calvary Presbyterian Church, San Francisco;
Past Interim President, San Francisco Theological Seminary

PREFACE

Psychospirituality is indispensable if you want to live fully your potentials. It needs to take roots in your personality, cultivated, and find expression in life. Thus, his book invites you to harness your psychospirituality to empower your life. It speaks to both Christians and lay readers who seek Christian precept to overcome helplessness in order to enhance emotional and spiritual growth. In our present materialistic world with a culture of unbelief, the life of Daniel of the Old Testament, as during his time, reminds you that a steadfast faith in God can be a bulwark of strength and a source of inspiration to others. Daniel's life is a testament that you, too, can foster a deeper level of personality development that reaches out like shining stars, to enlighten and influence the world around you. Hence, *Empowered* attempts an unprecedented exploration of the intersection of psychology and theology towards the psychospiritual study of a biblical character – the prophet Daniel of the Old Testament -- to answer two questions:

- How is psychospirituality expressed in Daniel's life and empowered him?
- How can you apply the lessons to empower your life?

The result is an enhanced understanding of Daniel, the person; how his personality interplays with divine calling; and 10 practical lessons backed by research findings that can better your life.

I am a board-certified psychiatrist of Christian faith who is deeply interested in seeking spiritual truths and to apply psychospiritual principles in patient's care, particularly to persons of faith. I'm not a theologian, although I have long engaged in the serious study of the Bible. This book represents my personal reflection on the book of Daniel. I feel that with psychiatry seemingly focusing primarily on the biological aspects of the mind and brain, and Christians not paying enough attention to the psychological nuances of the scriptures, psychiatry seems to have lost its soul while theology couldn't find its mind. This book attempts to connect the two disciplines more intimately through the study of Daniel and the integration of sound research findings with scriptural truths to empower your life.

The book consists of 3 parts:

- Part 1 describes Daniel's encounters with the Babylonian and Persian kings. They represent Daniel's conscious psychospiritual experience.
- Part 2 depicts Daniel's dream and visions. They represent Daniel's unconscious psychospiritual experience.
- Part 3 provides Daniel's 10 lessons by which you can empower your life.

At the end of each chapter, key points are summarized. A glossary clarifies key concepts. Tables and figures are meant to facilitate understanding of the background and scriptural context of the book of Daniel. Research issues, including methodological approach and the definition of psychospirituality are appended so that readers can focus right away on Daniel's experience.

HOW TO USE THIS BOOK

Here are some suggestions on how you can use materials from each of the 12 chapters of Daniel and his 10 lessons:

- Reading materials for quiet time and meditation.
- Reference for Bible study on Daniel.
- Course material for adult Sunday school.

- Discussion topics for group Bible study.
- Sermon subjects for preachers and pastors.
- Materials for undergraduate course on psychospirituality.
- Graduate research course on psychospirituality.
- Research materials for positive psychology and psychiatry.
- Case and reference material for self-help groups.
- Motivational materials for people considering changing behavioral patterns.
- Faith-based materials for persons in therapy.
- Advice for healthy living.

Although the book could enhance your emotional and spiritual growth, it is not intended to replace therapy. Those who need psychological help should consult professionals or continue therapy.

The inspiration in writing this book originates from the UCSF Christian Evangelistic Fellowship where I serve as a spiritual advisor. I am indebted to the Rev. Dr. James Emerson and Sara Charles, M.D. for their continuing support. Stanley Sue, PhD gave useful suggestions and encouragement. Walter R. Hearn provided helpful feedback about the manuscript. Owen Wolkowitz, M.D., generously shared his data on telomere and telomerase that contributed to the ideas of chapter 21. As usual, my wife, Tina, has been most patient through out this project. To her, I dedicate this book and my abiding love. Finally, to Christ, whose words and life example, continues to inspire in many amazing ways and deepen my conviction of who He is--praise be to Him, to God the Father, and to the Holy Spirit.

Albert C. Gaw, M.D.

INTRODUCTION

*E*mpowerment is a process by which you gain mastery over your affairs.[1] It is a positive and dynamic process that focuses on your strength, rights and capabilities. There are many advantages to be empowered, including better quality of life, and mastery over illnesses.[2] This book explores how psychospirituality could empower you.

WHY DANIEL?

Searching for an example of a psychospiritually-empowered person, I turned to the Bible. Yet, selecting an empowered Olympian among the numerous heroes in both the Old and New Testament is not an easy task. After careful consideration of the personal qualities of psychospirituality that is the focus of this book, I recommend the prophet Daniel of the Old Testament for the following reasons:

- First, compared to the other heroes of the Old Testament, from the patriarch--Abraham, Isaac, and Jacob; to the monarchs--King Saul, King David, King Solomon; and the prophets--Isaiah, Jeremiah, Ezekiel, Jonah, and others; Daniel's life stands out as most nearly flawless in personality make-up, skilled in interpersonal relation, having a steadfast faith in God, and unmatched passion to serve his people. His life exudes confidence, strong will, cool under fire, wisdom, love, faith, hope, resilience, and decisiveness – attributes of authentic psychospirituality.

- Second, beyond the personality factor, events in the Bible attest to the reaches of Daniel's psycho-spiritual power. As a young Jew exiled to Babylon, Daniel was able to attain a high political position in King Nebuchadnezzar's court. His spirituality, skill in dream interpretation and statesmanship contributed to his long career beginning from Babylonian King Nebuchadnezzar's era and lasting into the early years of Persian King Cyrus's reign. For seventy years of the Jewish Diaspora in Babylon, he and his friends were steadfast figures who were instrumental in sustaining and preserving the faith and culture of his people. Daniel's dream experience and visions predicted the rise and fall of the great empires of Babylon, Persia, Greece and Rome. They foretold the coming of the Messiah and events at the end of the world. During the oppressive reign of Antiochus IV Epiphanes (175-164 B.C.), the story of his steadfast faith and that of his three compatriots have provided comfort, encouragement, hope, and inspiration to his people. Christ referred to Daniel's statement of the "abomination that causes desolation" (Daniel 11:31) when he discussed the signs of the end of the age (Matthew 24:15; Luke 21:20). The resurrection of the dead in the Bible was first mentioned in Daniel (Daniel 12:13). Events in the Book of Revelation (1:7, 5:11, 13:5-8) referenced Daniel's vision (1:1; 7:10; 7:8,11, 21). It was during Daniel's stewardship in King Cyrus's reign that the first group of Jewish exiles was allowed to return to Judah and rebuild Jerusalem. Thus, the book of Daniel is critical in connecting events from the Old Testament to the New. It predicted the destiny of the world. And it carries weighty spiritual lessons.

- Third, the book of Daniel contains robust and exquisite details about his life that facilitate research. The book documented his dream and prophetic visions, as well as his emotional reactions to these events that provided insight into his personality. We also have the benefit of historical and cultural materials to help you understand what factors may have shaped and influenced Daniel's personality, his actions, and motives. By unraveling the secret of his personality and spirituality, you can learn how it empowered him, and can consider how the lessons may apply to your life.

DANIEL, THE MAN AND HIS TIME

Daniel's psychospiritual experiences were recorded in 12 chapters, divided almost equally into two sections. The first section (chapters 1-6) was made up primarily of historical narratives (NIV Study Bible, 1318). Chapter 2:4 to chapter 7 were originally written in Aramaic, the common Chaldean language of the time. They addressed primarily the gentile audience. The chapters documented Daniel's objective behavioral experience and that of his three young friends at the gentile kings' court. They dealt with overt conflicts, adjustments, coping and trials of the young Jewish exiles with their gentile captors. These narratives were Daniel's conscious, objective experiences. From a psycho-spiritual perspective and for the purpose of our study, we shall group them as Daniel's "objective manifestation of his character and psychospirituality."

The second section (chapters 7-12) was chiefly eschatological in theological content (1318). Chapter 7 was still written in Aramaic, although it began to address Israeli's concern. Chapters 8-12 were written in Hebrew and were focused on the nation of Israel. They contained Daniel's dreams and visions that were interpreted to him by angelic media. These dreams and visions were very private and Daniel narrated them in the first person's perspective. They described the trials of the nation of Israel in the gentile world. They predicted the rise and fall of the great empires during Daniel's time and those that were to come. They also included Daniel's detailed emotional reactions to these events. You will note that his emotional reaction to these events stood in stark contrast to the demeanor of his objective behavioral encounter when he faced Babylonian and Persian kings. I believe the contrast suggested hidden spiritual meaning and revealed critical aspects of Daniel's character and spirituality that can easily escape your attention. Because these dream and visions most likely involved Daniel's unconscious mind and were meant to be Daniel's private revelations, we shall group them as Daniel's "subjective manifestations of his character and psychospirituality."

The timeline of Daniel's psycho-spiritual experience is depicted in figure 1.

Figure 1. Timeline of Daniel's ministry and related events (number in parenthesis indicates chapter in Daniel)

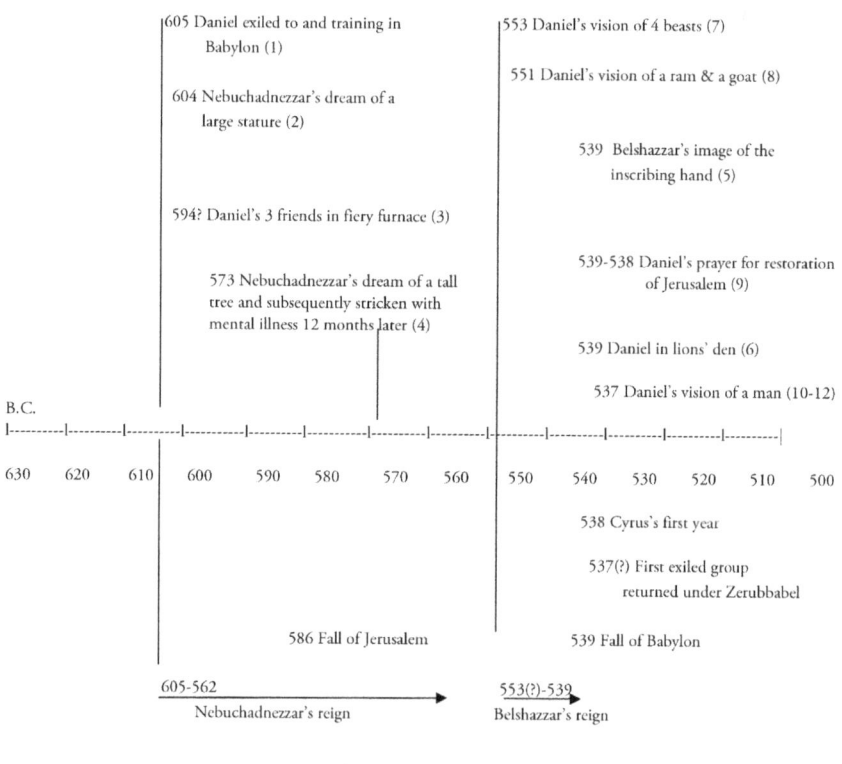

Source. *Adapted from* Zondervan NIV Study Bible (Fully Revised), Copyright© 1985.1995,2002 by Zondervan. 1320-1340.

HISTORICAL BACKGROUND

In the 6th century B.C., the nation of Israel, situated at the eastern Mediterranean coastal region, was caught up in the political struggle that pitched powerful Babylonia in the East against Egypt in the South. To survive, the kings of Judah had to carefully navigate her political alliance between these two superpowers (2 Kings 24-25; 2 Chronicles 36). When Jehoiakim, king of Judah, initially a vassal of Babylonian King Nebuchadnezzar II (609-562 B.C.E.) for three years, (2 Kings 24:1) rebelled against him, Nebuchadnezzar invaded Judah, captured Jehoiakim, and brought him, along with articles from the temple, to Babylon (Daniel 1:1-2). Daniel and his three compatriots were presumed to be among this first group of exile.

Young Jehoiachin (609-562 B.C.) succeeded his father as king of Judah. When King Jehoiachin surrendered to King Nebuchadnezzar II (609-562 B.C.) during a second siege of Jerusalem, the surrender was a crushing defeat for the people of Israel. Jehoiachin was taken in captivity into Babylon, along with all the treasures from the temple of Jerusalem, and ten thousand Jews including all the officers, fighting men, craftsmen, and artisans (2 Kings 24:12-16). Jerusalem and its temple, the grand house of worship Solomon built and the jewel of Jewish pride and holiness, now was in gentile's hand.

Table 1 provides key historical events of the Jewish captivity experience in Babylon and early Persia. You will note that the timing of the testing of the caliber of Daniel's character and faith and that of his friends were clustered around periods of transition of great empires, time fraught with uncertainty, turmoil, and extreme danger. (See also figure 1) Each chapter of Daniel's book constituted a trial that tested Daniel's psychospirituality. Through the triumph over these life's crises, Daniel's character and spirituality were revealed. The historical timing added to the urgency of the spiritual message that the author had intended to convey.

As a young exiled Jew in a gentile land, the fact that Daniel was able to attain and maintain a high political position in

Nebuchadnezzar's court, and continued his long service into the early Persian regime was an amazing personal achievement. Daniel lived to a ripe old age. How he was able to survive in such a highly visible, complex, sensitive, hostile, and foreign environment was an abject lesson in itself that had contemporary implications on how to navigate in such challenging situations.

With these backdrops in mind, we shall now examine Daniel's psychospirituality.

Table 1. Chronology of significant events during Daniel's ministry

Empire	King	Approximate Dates in B.C.	Significant Event(s)
Judah	Jehoiakim of Judah (609-598 B.C.)	609-598 605	Reign of Jehoiakim, king of Judah. Nebuchadnezzar defeated the Egyptian army at Carchemish. Jehoiakim transferred allegiance to Nebuchadnezzar but later rebelled and again allied with Egypt. Nebuchadnezzar sent a punitive army
	Jehoiachin	597	against him and conquered all of the "Hatti-country" which included the "city of Judah." The first exile including Daniel and his 3 friends were deported to Babylon

			Nebuchadnezzar took Jehoiakim's son Jehoiachin into captivity along with ten thousand persons.
	Zedekiah	597-586	Reign of Zedekiah, installed by Nebuchadnezzar as king of Judah. Zedekiah rebelled against Nebuchadnezzar. Nebuchadnezzar besieged Jerusalem. King Zedekiah escaped with his army in the evening but the Babylonian army overtook them. He was enucleated at Riblah and taken to Babylon. Nebuchadnezzar ordered Jerusalem destroyed in 586 B.C.
Babylonia	Nebuchadnezzar II	605-562	Nebuchadnezzar's reign
		604	Nebuchadnezzar's dream of an awesome statue

		597	Nebuchadnezzar took Jehoiakim's son Jehoiachin into captivity along with ten thousand persons.
		594	Daniel's 3 friends in fiery furnace
		586	Nebuchadnezzar captured King Zedekiah of Judah
		586	Fall of Jerusalem
		573	Nebuchadnezzar's dream of a tall tree and was subsequently stricken with a rare mental illness
		566	Recovery of Nebuchadnezzar from mental illness and restoration of his kingship 7 years later
Nabonidus		556-539	Nabonidus's reign
Belshazzar (Co-regency with Nabonidus) (553-539 B.C.)		553	Daniel's dream and vision of 4 beasts
		551 539	Daniel's dream of a Ram and Goat Belshazzar's image of the inscribing hand

Persia	Cyrus the Great (559-530 B.C.)	539	Daniel in the lion's den
		538	
			Daniel's prayer for restoration of Jerusalem and
		537	the vision of "Seventy Seven"
		537 ?	Daniel's vision of a man; the kings of the south and north.
			Cyrus issued decree allowing the first exiled group's returns under Zerubbabel

Source. *Adapted from* Zondervan NIV Study Bible (Fully Revised), Copyright© 1985, 1995, 2002 by Zondervan), 571-572, 1320-1340.

PART 1

**Encounter with the Babylonian
and Persian Kings:**

**The Objective Manifestation of
Daniel's Psychospirituality**

CHAPTER 1

To Eat or not to Eat the King's Food: The First Test of Daniel's Psychospirituality

Daniel resolved not to defile himself with the
royal food and wine (Daniel 1:8)

King Nebuchadnezzar wanted to pick some young Jews to serve in his court. Daniel and his companions were selected because they fitted the king's specifications: of royal family and nobility, without physical defect, handsome, with aptitude for learning, well informed, and quick to understand (Daniel 1:3-4; table 2). But first, Daniel and his friends had to be acculturated into the Babylonian culture. They had to learn its language, literature and the art of understanding visions and dream interpretation. Even their identities had to be changed: Daniel's name (God is [my] Judge") was changed to Belteshazzar "Bel (i.e., Marduk), protect his life"); Hananiah ("The Lord shows grace") to Shadrach ("command of Aku [Sumerian moon-god]"); Mishael ("who is what God is") to Meshach ("who is what Aku is"); and Azariah ("the Lord helps") to Abednego ("servant of Nego/Nebo [i.e., Nabu]").[3] The name change signified they were now assimilated into their foreign culture, subjected to

Nebuchadnezzar's authority, and at the mercy of his foreign gods.[4] Confronted with the humiliation of defeat and exiled to a foreign land, the Jewish people had to find ways to adjust to a foreign culture while maintaining their core heritage and identity. And the adjustment wasn't easy.

In preparation for their services to the king's court, Daniel and his friends were trained for three years before being interviewed by the king. As part of the training program, Daniel and his friends were given a daily portion of the royal food and drink. It was a routine matter for most captives. In fact, the opportunity to partake of the best Babylonian food and wine could be seen as a privilege and a luxury. Certainly it was more expedient and easy for Daniel to say yes to the challenge of the appetite of the flesh. Why not act like the Babylonians did while in Babylon? As Jews, however, the food from Nebuchadnezzar's table was considered "contaminated" [not kosher] because it had been offered to idols; the wine was probably poured out on a pagan altar; and ceremonially unclean animals were used and prepared not according to Mosaic laws.[5] At stake was not simply the clash of food and eating habits of two cultures. Eating food prepared according to Mosaic laws was a ritualistic symbol of the covenantal injunction between God and the Israelites to act according to what the Lord had prescribed for his chosen people to separate themselves as "holy people of God" from pagans who worshipped idols made by human hands and of human materials (Deuteronomy 29:9-18). Was Daniel going to compromise his faith?

Daniel said no. "Daniel resolved not to defile himself with the royal food and wine, and he asked the chief official for permission not to defile himself this way" (Daniel 1:8; See also chapter 13). Regardless of the potential consequences that could befall him including the deprivation of a life of luxury and a chance to serve in the king's court, and even possibly inviting death for defying the king's order, Daniel was not going to defile the name of God and go against the covenant God had made with his people by eating contaminated food. He was determined not to compromise his spirituality and faith.

But Daniel had to find a way to convince his captors the merit of his decision. So Daniel proposed to the guard to settle a matter of faith. He asked that he and his friends be permitted to eat only a vegetable diet and drink water for ten days. Afterward, the guard could judge for himself their physical appearances against those of the rest of the young men who would be eating the prescribed food and wine.

This episode was a crude scientific experiment designed with a comparison group. But it reflects Daniel's logical and scientific mind-set. The boldness of the proposal reveals his faith and spirituality. He believed if he took the Word of God seriously, God would positively respond to him. He had complete faith in God. And Daniel's faith experiment proved efficacious. At the end of ten days, he and his four companions "looked healthier and better nourished than any of the young men who ate the royal food" (Daniel 1:15). So they were allowed to continue their vegetarian diet. When they were presented to King Nebuchadnezzar three years later, the king found none equal to Daniel and his friends. Not only did they excel in physical appearance, but in every matter of wisdom and understanding, the king found them ten times better than all the magicians and enchanters in the Babylonian kingdom (Daniel 1:19,20). Daniel and his friends kept faith in God, and God did not fail them.

In this test of spirituality in the choice of food, you can already discern how young Daniel exercised judgment that reflects the basic value of his belief. He would apply spiritual wisdom and earthly knowledge to cope with matters of faith and sensitive political situations. The man of God knew how to operate in a heathen world, with wisdom, tact, consideration of others, sensitivity, and persuasiveness, yet impart a cool confidence that reflected the authenticity of his beliefs and the principles of his faith. Early in life, Daniel already had set his mind to seek God's will and obey His commands. This key character trait helped distinguish Daniel from other mortals and may point to the secret of Daniel's psychospirituality that made him esteemed by God.

Because Daniel kept faith in God and remained spiritually faithful to the Lord, the Lord gave him, "knowledge and understanding of all kinds of literature and learning. And Daniel could understand visions and dreams of all kinds" (Daniel 1:17). Daniel's spiritual wisdom and earthly knowledge were to prove instrumental later in saving him and his friends' lives. They were pivotal in serving his people as well.

The food was the first test of Daniel's spirituality and Daniel passed with flying colors. Clarence McCartney said it well.

> The grandest thing that the sun that day looked down on in Babylon, the most royal bit of furniture about the court of Nebuchadnezzar, the noblest creature in God's universe, was a man with a moral purpose, an immortal soul, taking his quiet stand for righteousness, with time, circumstance, expediency, the appetites of the flesh, the chances of promotion, the will of the potentate of the whole earth, personal safety, all leading and urging in the other direction; and yet overcoming all these influences was a moral purpose, and a decision of the soul.[6]

Because Daniel remained faithful to God in a relatively small matter reflected in the choice of food, we shall now see how God entrusted him with bigger responsibilities.

Table 2. Descriptions given to Daniel and their references

Source	Descriptive Quotes	Reference
King Nebuchadnezzar's specification of qualified candidate	"Of royal family and nobility, young man without physical defect, handsome, showing aptitude for learning, well-informed, quick to understand, qualified to serve in the king's court."	Chap 1:3-4

Chief Official	Gave Daniel ("God is [my] judge") new Babylonian name: Belteshazzar probably meant "Bel (i.e., Marduk), protects his life!"	Chap 1:7 and Study note 1:7
God	"God gave knowledge and understanding of all kinds of literature and learning. And Daniel could understand visions and dreams of all kinds."	Chap 1:17
King Nebuchadnezzar	"…he found none equal to Daniel, Hananiah, Michael and Azariah; …In every matter of wisdom and understanding about which the king questioned them, he found them ten times better than all the magicians and enchanters in his whole kingdom."	Chap 1:19-20
Arioch, commander of the king's guard	"I have found a man among the exiles from Judah who can tell the king what his dream means."	Chap 2:25
King Nebuchadnezzar	"Surely your God is the God of gods, and the Lord of kings and a revealer of mysteries, for you were able to reveal this mystery."	Chap 2:47
King Nebuchadnezzar	"I know that the spirit of the holy gods is in you, and no mystery is too difficult for you."	Chap 4:9
Queen at King Belshazzar's court	"There is a man in your kingdom who has the spirit of the holy gods in him. In the time of your father he was found to have insight and intelligence and wisdom like that of the gods… This man Daniel…was found to have a keen mind and knowledge, and also	Chap 5:11-12

	the ability to interpret dreams, explain riddles, and solve difficult problems."	
Darius the Medes	"Daniel so distinguished himself among the administrators and the satraps by his exceptional qualities that the king planned to set him over the whole kingdom."	Chap 6:3
Darius' administrators and satraps	"...the administrators and the satraps tried to find grounds for charges against Daniel in the conduct of government affairs, but they were unable to do so. They could find no corruption in him, because he was trustworthy and neither corrupt nor negligent... we will never find any basis for charges against this man Daniel unless it has something to do with the law of his God."	Chap 6:4-5
The angel Gabriel	"Daniel, I have now come to give you insight and understanding. As soon as you began to pray, an answer was given, which I have come to tell you, for you are highly esteemed."	Chap 9:22-23
Gabriel	"Daniel, you who are highly esteemed...Since the day you set your mind to gain understanding and to humble yourself before your God, your words were heard, and I have come to respond to them."	Chap 10:11-12
A man dressed in linen	"...You will rest, and then at the end of the days you will rise to receive your allotted inheritance."	Chap 12:13

Source. *Adapted from* Zondervan NIV Study Bible (Fully Revised) Copyright© 1985, 1995, 2002 by Zondervan.

Chapter 1. KEY POINTS

1. Early in his life, Daniel determined to align key life decisions with the value of his faith in God. In turn, God gave him wisdom, knowledge, and skill to understand all kinds of visions and dreams.

2. Daniel's character and spirituality were shown by the resoluteness and courage in how and why he chose to adhere to the principles of his faith by refusing to eat the king's food and wine, which he considered "contaminated" according to the Mosaic law.

3. Daniel's skillful interaction with the guard reflected his wisdom and psychospirituality. His proposal for an experiment with a controlled group to convince the guard the merit of eating a vegetarian diet indicated the presence of a scientific mind-set.

4. Psychospirituality that stems from a clear understanding of and acting according to the principles of your faith can empower you. It enables you to say no to things that are harmful to you, make wise choices for your health, avoid temptations, cultivate a winning personality, live a righteous life, and obtain wisdom.

CHAPTER 2

To Do Or Not Do The Impossible: The Second Test Of Daniel's Psychospirituality

…there is a God in heaven who reveals mysteries (Daniel 2:27)

Young Daniel's spirituality was severely tested when called on to interpret King Nebuchadnezzar's forgotten dream. He also had to be very tactful in handling the politics in the king's court and in conveying the interpretation of the dream to the king.

Nebuchadnezzar had a troubling dream he couldn't remember. He summoned his magicians, enchanters, sorcerers and astrologers to tell what it was. If they could, they would be richly rewarded and honored. If not, they would all be killed and their houses destroyed. And the king was a man who would not take no for an answer.

You could sense the consternation of the Babylonian wise men. Though with the best earthly knowledge and skill of telling, they were totally helpless and unable to interpret dream without first knowing the content. There is a limit to earthly knowledge and ability. In desperation, they pleaded with the king to tell them his dream. But they got a royal rebuff and were accused of conspiring to tell misleading and wicked things. In exasperation, they explained to Nebuchadnezzar what he didn't want to hear--what he asked for was too difficult and unreasonable. "No one can reveal it to the king except gods that do not live among men" (Daniel 2:11).

Furious, the king ordered the execution of all the wise men. Although Daniel and his friends were not present in the court when the king issued his edict, as wise men, they, too, would become victims of circumstances.

Daniel learned from Arioch, the commander of the king's guard, why the king made such a harsh and fateful decision. He immediately went to the king and asked for time so that he might interpret the dream for him. That was a bold and desperate move for Daniel. Although Daniel had received Babylonian training in dream interpretation, he hadn't been tested. Faced with the same dilemma as the Babylonian wise men--not knowing the content of the king's dream--would Daniel be able to tell what the king's dream was? The stakes were extremely high for Daniel. The lives of all wise men in Babylon and their families, Daniel's life and that of his three companions hung on his ability to divine and interpret the king's dream. If he failed, the history of Israel might have turned out differently. Who would plead with God and perhaps influence the gentile Persian king to allow the Jews to return to Judah and rebuild Jerusalem after seventy years of exile, thereby fulfilling Jeremiah's prophecy? (See chapter 9) If the mystery of the king's dream could only be revealed by gods who do not live among men, could Jehovah, Israel's God, be counted on to show Himself to be superior to all the Babylonian gods? Daniel was confronted with a test of faith of epic proportion. Could he deliver? Or more important, could his God be counted on to reveal the dream to him?

Daniel explained the urgent matter to his three companions and urged them to pray to God for mercy concerning this mystery so they could be spared death. They fervently petitioned God.

Consequently, God revealed the mystery of the king's dream to Daniel in a vision at night. Daniel was elated. He praised God and affirmed Jehovah God as the source of all wisdom and power, the one who reveals deep and hidden things to the wise and the discerning (Daniel 2:20-22).

> Praise be to the name of God for ever and ever; wisdom and power are his...
> He gives wisdom to the wise and knowledge to the discerning...
> I thank and praise you, O God of my Fathers:
> You have given me wisdom and power, you have made known to me what we
> asked of you, you have made known to us the dream of the king.

Daniel was a wise and discerning man. He knew the limitation of earthly training and knowledge. He turned to God when it really counts. With critical matters involving revelation, Daniel understood that only the one and living God has the power to reveal them. And God chooses to reveal it to the person(s) and at His own time.

DANIEL'S POLITICAL ASTUTENESS

With the slightest provocation, Nebuchadnezzar would order men killed. Though Daniel now knew the king's dream, how should he convey it to the king? How he handled this sensitive matter also revealed his spirituality, and is a lesson on Politics 101 for modern believers. Let's see how he did it.

Daniel could have approach the king directly, told the king his dream and got all the credit he deserved. Instead, he went first to Arioch, the commander of the king's guard, who was appointed by the king to carry out the execution order. Daniel asked him not to execute the wise men. Instead, to take him to the king so that he could interpret the king's dream.

This was a smart political move. For Daniel to survive in an alien court, he needed the support of Arioch and the Babylonian wise men. If Daniel could save their lives, he would have won over the esteem and allegiance of his Babylonian colleagues. By approaching Arioch first, Daniel credited him for facilitating the divination of the king's dream. It was a win-win situation for Arioch, the wise men, and Daniel.

Daniel wanted to tell the king that Jehovah is superior to all the Babylonian gods. He had to be very careful not to offend the king's beliefs. The scripture described his tactful conversation with the king.

> No wise men, enchanter, magician, or diviner can explain to the king the mystery he has asked about, but there is a God in heaven who reveals mysteries. He has shown King Nebuchadnezzar what will happen in days to come (Daniel 2:27-28).

> As for me, this mystery has been revealed to me, not because I have greater wisdom than other living men, but so that you, O king, may know the interpretation and that you may understand what went through your mind (Daniel 3:30).

Daniel then went on to tell and interpret the king's dream.

> You looked, O king, and there before you stood a large statue–an enormous, dazzling statue, awesome in appearance. The head of the statue was made of pure gold, its chest and arms of silver, its belly and thighs of bronze, its legs of iron, its feet partly of iron and partly of baked clay. While you were watching, a rock was cut out, but not by human hands. It struck the statue on its feet of iron and clay and smashed them. Then the iron, the clay, the bronze, the silver and the gold were broken to pieces at the same time and became like chaff on a threshing floor in the summer. The wind swept them away without leaving

a trace. But the rock that struck the statue became a huge mountain and filled the whole earth (Daniel 3:31-35) (See also figure 2).

Daniel went on to interpret the dream.

> You, O king, are the king of kings. The God of heaven has given you dominion and power and might and glory; in your hands he has placed mankind and the beasts of the field and the birds of the air. Whether they live, he has made you ruler over them all. You are that head of gold.

> After you, another kingdom will rise, inferior to yours. Next a third kingdom, one of bronze, will rule over the whole earth. Finally, there will be a fourth kingdom, strong as iron—for iron breaks and smashes everything—and as iron breaks things into pieces, so it will crush and break all the others. Just as you saw that the feet and toes were partly of basked clay and partly iron, so that this will be a divided kingdom; yet it will have some strength of iron in it, even as you saw iron mixed with clay. As the toes were partly iron and partly clay, so this kingdom will be partly strong and partly brittle. And just as you saw the iron mixed with baked clay, so the people will be a mixture and will not remain united, any more than iron mixes with the clay.

> In the time of these kings, the God of heaven will set up a kingdom that will never be destroyed, nor will it be left to another people. It will crush all these kingdoms and bring them to an end, but it will itself endure forever. This is the meaning of the vision of the rock cut out of a mountain, but not by human hands—a rock that broke the iron, the bronze, the clay, the silver and the gold to pieces. (Daniel 3:37-45) (See table 3)

Table 3. Nebuchadnezzar's dream of a big statue and its corresponding representations in Daniel's vision of the four beasts, and a ram and a goat

Huge Statue[1]	Four Beasts[2]	A Ram and a Goat[3]	Identified Empire	Chronology of Major Empires
Head of Gold	Lion		Babylon (Da 2:37-38)	Babylonia 626-539 B.C.
Chest and Arms of silver	Bear	Ram	Medo-Persia (Da. 8:20)	Medo-Persia 539-330 B.C.
Belly and Thighs of Bronze	Leopard	Goat	Greece (Da. 8:21)	Greece 330-63 B.C.
Leg of Iron	Terrifying and Frightening Beast		Rome	Rome 63 B.C. – 100 A.D.
Feet of Clay and Iron Mixed	↓		↓	↓
Rock that Struck the Stature			Kingdom of Heaven	End of Time

Source. *Adapted from* Zondervan NIV Study Bible and Notes. (Fully Revised), Copyright© 1985, 1995, 2002 by Zondervan), 1330.

[1] Nebuchadnezzar's dream interpreted by Daniel (Ch. 2)
[2] Daniel's dream/vision during Belshazzar's 1st year reign (Ch. 7)
[3] Daniel's vision during Belshazzar's 3rd year reign (Ch.8)

Impressed, the mighty King Nebuchadnezzar prostrated before Daniel, paid him honor, ordered an offering and incense be presented to him, and made him ruler over the entire province of Babylon and in charge of all the wise men (Daniel 2:46). The king also acknowledged that Daniel's God is the God of gods and the Lord of kings and a revealer of mysteries (Daniel 2:47).

In a further astute political move, Daniel requested the king to appoint his three friends, administrators over the province of Babylon. He strengthened his political office by having his trusted and able friends placed in positions of power, while he remained in the court to serve the king.

God was preeminent in Daniel's life. Daniel had an acute awareness of the needs of the people around him. He saw clearly the big pictures and easily distinguished the forests from the trees. Through all circumstances, he knew how to win over the respect and allegiance of the people around him, a skill necessary for survival in a hostile land. Daniel's action glorified God's name in a gentile land.

Chapter 2. KEY POINTS

1. Daniel's psychospirituality faced a critical test when he was confronted with a life-and-death decision on whether he could divine and interpret King Nebuchadnezzar's forgotten dream.

2. Daniel knew in matter of revelation, only God has the power to reveal it. He realized the limit of human knowledge and training and how and when to turn to God for revelation.

3. Daniel's unwavering faith in God who answers prayers and petitions was a source of his psychospiritual strength and power.

4. Daniel had committed and like-minded prayer partners who could pray with him in times of crisis.

5. Daniel's character exuded courage, cool under fire, humility, generosity and wisdom. He was magnanimous even to his potential enemies and competitors and knew how to win them over.

CHAPTER 3

To Die Or Not To Die For One's Beliefs:
The Trial Of Daniel's Three Friends' Faith

They trusted in him [Jehovah] and defied the king's command
and were willing to give up their lives rather than serve or
worship any god except their own God (Daniel 3:28)

I n this episode, Daniel's three friends' faith was severely tested.
Although Daniel was not directly involved, the fact that he
would face a similar trial of his faith late in his life (See chapter
6) indicates how vulnerable the exiled Jews were to the jealous plots
of the foreign wise men. The trial of his friends was an omen to
Daniel. Earlier, we saw how his friends who were appointed to key
governmental positions protected Daniel. It stands to reason that if
the Babylonian wise men could strip away that protective shield from
Daniel, would he be safe from their next move?

The opportunity to set a trap against Daniel's friends came up
when proud Nebuchadnezzar made a huge image of gold of him and

decreed that everybody in his land must worship it upon hearing the sounds of music or be immediately thrown into the blazing furnace (Daniel 3:5-6).

When Daniel's friends, Shadrach, Meshach and Abednego, defied the king's order, the accusers brought them before the king. The king confronted them with their defiance and warned them of its consequence. But they remained steadfastly defiant and boldly told the king, "If we are thrown into the blazing furnace, the God we serve is able to save us from it, and he will rescue us from your hands O King. But even if he does not, we want you to know, O king, that we will not serve your gods or worship the image of gold you have set up" (Daniel 3:17-18). They were ready to die for their faith and beliefs!

Who dared defy the king? The king exploded and ordered the furnace be heated seven times hotter, had the three men tied up, and thrown into the furnace. But the Lord performed a miracle. King Nebuchadnezzar saw "four men walking around in the fire, unbound and unharmed, and the fourth looks like a son of the gods" (Daniel 3:25). He quickly ordered the three men be brought out. When they were completely unharmed, the king was totally amazed. The power and saving grace of God so impressed the king that he decreed--"the people of any nation or language who say anything against the God of Shadrach, Meshach and Abednego be cut into pieces and their houses be turned into piles of rubble, for no other god can save this way" (Daniel 3:29). In an ironic twist of events, what was a spiritual and political crisis for the three men and the Jewish people turned unexpectedly favorable to their cause. God intervened in time just when his people needed it. God kept His part of the bargain when the three young men honored Him. By remaining steadfast in their faith even in the face of death, the Lord delivered and saved Daniel's friends. In turn, the Lord's name was institutionalized and elevated throughout Babylon. The king also promoted the three men to even higher position in Babylon.

As a result, Daniel's political position was further strengthened. How were his friends able to stand so resolutely on a matter of faith when facing death? This episode is reminiscence of the test of food in chapter one. Clarence McCartney was of the opinion that Daniel's resoluteness on food must have emboldened them to also stand fast on their faith.[7] Daniel's action shows you the power of modeling. The deep faith that resonated among the foursome young men is inspiring and a delight to behold. Influenced by Daniel, his three friends displayed unshakeable faith in God, and God rescued and rewarded them.

Chapter 3. KEY POINTS

1. The testing of Daniel's friends' faith was an indirect challenge to Daniel's psychospirituality and position.

2. Daniel's friends defied the king's order to worship his golden idol. As a result, they were thrown into the fiery furnace.

3. God performed a miracle. The king saw 4 persons walking in the furnace unbound and unharmed. The fourth person looked like "a son of the gods." The king was totally impressed with Jehovah's might and he elevated and institutionalized Jehovah's name in Babylon.

4. How his friends most likely modeled their faith and courage after Daniel revealed Daniel's psychospirituality.

CHAPTER 4

To Humble Or Not Humble Before God: The Tall Tree Cut Down – The Humbling Of King Nebuchadnezzar

Those who walk in pride he is able to humble (Daniel 4:37)

Despite Nebuchadnezzar's earlier experience with Daniel concerning his dream (chapter 2) and witnessing the miracle that saved Daniel's three friends from the fiery furnace (chapter 3), the king remained arrogant. God made Nebuchadnezzar insane to teach him a lesson of humility. King Nebuchadnezzar himself narrated the episode after he recovered from a mental illness.

The king had another dream and the images and visions that passed through his mind terrified him. In his vision, he saw an enormous tall tree that grew and touched the sky…Then a holy messenger came down from heaven and shouted to cut down the tree. He further said that the mind of that person will be changed to that of an animal, and predicted that "until seven times pass by for him" before his recovery. (Daniel 4:10-16) (See table 4)

King Nebuchadnezzar remembered his dream this time. When all the Babylonian magicians, enchanters, astrologers and diviners couldn't divine his dream, Daniel was again called upon to interpret. Having the benefit of knowing the king's dream, Daniel's task was made easier. But Daniel still had to be very careful in how he conveyed the interpretation to the king, as the dream carried an injunction and a warning: the king must repent or he may face the prospect of becoming insane. This was extremely sensitive to bring up with an arrogant and bad-temper potentate. How would Daniel handle this? Daniel was straightforward. His boldness and candidness may reflect the trusting relationship Daniel had formed with the king. Daniel had correctly interpreted the king's past dream, and he handled the presentation with tact and diplomacy. Daniel served diligently and uprightly in his service to the king. The king trusted him. So Daniel warned him, "The tall tree was the king." Unless he "renounce his sins by doing what is right, and his wickedness by being kind to the oppressed" (Daniel 4:27), as the messenger in the dream decreed, he will become insane and be driven away from his people and live like an animal. "Seven times [seven years] will pass by until the king acknowledges that the Most High is sovereign over the kingdoms of men and gives them to anyone he wishes." If the king renounced his sins by doing what was right and abandoned his wickedness by being kind to the oppressed, his prosperity may continue (Daniel 4:24-27). The Bible didn't record the king's immediate response. But twelve months later, while he was boasting about his great empire and of his mighty power, he suddenly developed a mental illness scholars labeled as "boantrophy"[8], in which his mind and behavior were transformed into that of an animal. As a result, he was driven away from his people. [Seven years] passed before his sanity was restored and he returned to his throne. The king then made the following proclamation concerning Jehovah God.

> His dominion is an eternal dominion;
> His kingdom endures from generation to generation.
> All the peoples of the earth are regarded as nothing.

He does as he pleases with the powers of heaven and the
people of the earth,
No one can hold back his hand or say to him: "What have
you done?" (Daniel 4:34-35)

This was quite a humbling acknowledgment of Jehovah's power
and His kingdom coming from the lips of the king of kings. It took
the episode of a severe mental illness to humble the king. From a
modern psychiatric perspective, did Nebuchadnezzar suffer from a
megalomaniacal psychotic break, an acute attack of schizophrenia, or
a psychotic break with or without a mood disorder? We can only speculate. The description of his behavior with marked features of mental
deterioration, prolonged course of illness, and spontaneous recovery,
suggests an acute psychotic illness (DSM-IV-TR[9]). ["Boantrophy" is
not listed in any of the Diagnostic and Statistical Manuals (DSM) of
the American Psychiatric Association]. From the king's statement, he
must have experienced a change of heart, became humble, fulfilling
conditions mentioned by Daniel that could lead to his recovery. The
king said in his testimony.

> Now I, Nebuchadnezzar, praise and exalt and glorify the
> King of heaven, because everything he does is right and all
> his ways are just. And those who walk in pride he is able to
> humble (Daniel 4:37).

This episode of illness carries a strong moral and psychospiritual message. (See also chapter 16) Although you may intuitively
sense that some people may get sick mentally because of their morally depraved behavior, Nebuchadnezzar's illness is a rare recording
of a biblical episode in which the apparent precipitating cause of a
severe mental illness was attributed to a moral depravation of character and arrogance. The affinity to moral and spiritual issue suggests
a spiritual illness. This illness episode is reminiscent of other Old
Testament prophets' (Ezekiel, Jeremiah, etc.) pleas and warning to
the Israelites to repent and return to God. Proverbs says it well.

> "When pride comes, then comes disgrace, but with
> humility comes wisdom (Proverbs 11:2).

Before his downfall a man's heart is proud, but humility comes before honor (Proverbs 18:12).

This was the last recorded episode of Daniel's encounter with Nebuchadnezzar. It took the experience of the big statue (chapter 2), the miraculous rescue of Daniel's three friends from the furnace (chapter 3), and finally, the experience of a mental illness (chapter 4) to convince Nebuchadnezzar to turn from his ways to the Almighty Jehovah. Daniel and his friends' psychospirituality subdued the king who had conquered Judah and Jerusalem militarily. Although Daniel and his compatriots were captives in a gentile land, they emerged spiritually and politically stronger following their trials of faith. God deals fairly and justly with human being. As the score in Handel's *Messiah* sings,

> Every valley shall be raised up, every mountain and hill made low;
>
> The rough ground shall become level, and the rugged places a plain.
>
> And the glory of the Lord will be revealed, and all mankind together shall see it. (Isaiah 40:4-5)

Table 4. Daniel's interpretation of Nebuchadnezzar's dream of a tall tree

The Dream	Interpretation	Warning to the King	Fulfillment of Prophecy
A tall tree, in the middle of the land, grew large and strong. A Messenger from Heaven called in a loud voice: "Cut down the tree... but let the stump and its roots, bound with iron and bronze, remain in the ground... Let him be drenched with the dew of heaven, and let him live with the animals among the plants of the earth.	Tall tree-- King Nebuchadnezzar. Messenger from Heaven--decree from the Most High against the king: -Be driven away from the people and will live with wild animals— become insane. (Not mentioned but implied when dream was fulfilled later.) -Seven times— time that will pass until the king acknowledges that the Most High is sovereign over the kingdoms of men and that He gives them to anyone He wishes.	"Renounce your sins by doing what is right, and your wickedness by being kind to the oppressed." (Da.4:27)	Twelve months later, as he was walking on the roof of the royal palace and boasting of his power and glory, a voice from heaven decreed that his royal authority has been taken away from him; that he will be driven away from people and live with wild animals until seven times will pass by for him and until he acknowledges that the Most High is sovereign over the kingdoms of men and gives them to anyone he wishes. (Da. 4:28-32)

Let his mind be changed from that of a man and let him be given the mind of an animal, till seven times passed by for him." (Da. 4:10-16)	-Stump with roots—his kingdom will be restored when the king acknowledges that heavens rule.		He became insane (v.34) allegedly stricken by a mental illness known as *boanthropy* which causes the victim to assume the appearance, habits and posture of cattle.(v.33) (NIV footnote, 4:25).

The description: "His body was drenched with the dew of heaven until his hair grew like the feathers of an eagle, and his nails like the claws of a bird." (4:33)

At the end of time, his sanity was restored. (Spontaneous recovery?) His honor, splendor and throne were restored. He became even greater than before. Nebuchadnezzar then praised the King of Heaven. |

Source. *Adapted from* Zondervan NIV Study Bible (Fully Revised) and Study notes, Copyright© 1985, 1995, 2002 by Zondervan), 1321-1322.

Chapter 4. KEY POINTS

1. Despite God's warning through dream and Daniel's exhortation, King Nebuchadnezzar remained arrogant and unrepentant of his sins.

2. While boosting of his power and empire twelve months after the dream, he was suddenly stricken with a mental illness that made him think and behave like an animal.

3. Nebuchadnezzar apparently repented and recovered [seven years] later.

4. It took a personal tragedy to finally convince the King to be humble, and to repent his ways by doing what was right and being kind to the oppressed.

5. Daniel's psychospirituality enabled him to remain humble; formed trusting relationship with King Nebuchadnezzar; gave correct, tactful, and timely interpretation of the king's dream that resulted in the glorification of Jehovah's name.

CHAPTER 5

To Repent Or Not Repent One's Sin: Belshazzar's Vision – The Hand Writing On The Wall And The Demise Of Babylon

You did not honor the God who holds in his hand
your life and all your ways. Therefore he sent the hand
that wrote the inscription (Daniel 5:25-26)

This episode has a similar theme to that of chapter 4, the fall of an arrogant monarch. But the sin Belshazzar committed was more egregious than that of Nebuchadnezzar.

Belshazzar succeeded Nebuchadnezzar as king of Babylon. In a great banquet he gave for a thousand of his nobles, he brought out the gold and silver goblets Nebuchadnezzar had taken from the temple of Jerusalem; drank from them; praised the idol gods of gold, silver, bronze, iron, wood and stone; and blasphemed the Lord. Suddenly, the fingers of a human hand appeared on the plaster of the wall and wrote,

Mene, Mene, Tekel, Parsin

The king was terrified and called for his enchanters, astrologers and diviners to interpret the writings. When all of them couldn't read the writings, the king became more fearful. The queen remembered that during Nebuchadnezzar's reign, Daniel had the ability to interpret dream, so he was summoned. Daniel narrated the experience of Belshazzar's predecessor: how God deposed Nebuchadnezzar from his throne by turning his mind into that of an animal and was driven from the people until he acknowledged that the Most High God is sovereign. Then Daniel told Belshazzar's his transgression--despite his knowledge of what had happened to his predecessor he did not humble himself, but set himself up against the Lord of heaven. Worse, he publicly flaunted the holy objects taken from the temple of Jerusalem and made a mockery of Jehovah's might. So Daniel delivered the fateful message: God sent the hand that wrote the inscription on the wall. Daniel then interpreted the vision (See table 5) as follows:

> *Mene*: God had numbered the days of your reign and brought it to an end.
> *Tekel*: You have been weighed on the scales and found wanting.
> *Peres*: Your kingdom is divided and given to the Medes and Persians. (Daniel 5:26-28)

Daniel referenced Nebuchadnezzar's behavior when he spoke to Belshazzar. Although both kings were arrogant, the outcome of their transgression was different: Nebuchadnezzar had become insane and recovered. Belshazzar was assassinated that evening and the Babylonian empire came to an end.

How was Belshazzar's behavior different from his predecessor?

Nebuchadnezzar boasted of his empire and majesty. He did not renounce his sins by doing what was right nor did he relinquish his wickedness by being kind to the oppressed. (Daniel 4:27) He dreamed of a huge statue (chapter 2), with a head of gold that symbolized him and his empire, went on to build a gold status of him, and demanded everyone to worship it (chapter 3). He witnessed the might and saving grace of God that saved Daniel's friends from the fiery furnace (chapter 3). Though he had an intellectual knowledge of the power of God, his heart remained stubborn and unrepentant. It could be said that the king was arrogant but may be unaware of his unconscious narcissism (See chapter 13). When he sinned, he did not publicly and consciously flaunt the God of Israel, nor did he defile His sacred vessels. He did not blaspheme the Lord. His sin could be considered one of omission. So God taught him a lesson of humility by afflicting him with a mental illness. But God was still merciful to him (as symbolized in the dream by leaving him a stump on the ground from which the tree was allowed to grow). Fortunately, the king recovered in time to proclaim God's absolute sovereignty, and reclaimed his throne. But he had to be made to understand that God does what He pleases, and that God's eternal dominion endures over any earthly kingdom. And out of the mouth of the greatest ruler of the Babylonian empire, he proclaimed that God is great. (See chapter 4)

Belshazzar's behavior was different. In a delirious celebration at his great banquet, he took out the gold and silver goblets that Nebuchadnezzar had taken from the temple of Jerusalem. The king, his nobles, his wives and concubines all drank from them as they praised the idol gods. They publicly defiled the holy vessels of the Lord and made a mockery of Jehovah God.

Belshazzar knew what had happened to his predecessor, but he did not humble himself. Belshazzar consciously flouted against Jehovah, and therefore, his act was a sin of commission. That very night, the Bible recorded that King Belshazzar was assassinated and Darius the Medes took over the Babylonian empire (Daniel 5:30).

This episode reminds us once more the lesson of humility. (See also chapter 16) Pride can cause the downfall of both mighty man and nation. Unless proud leaders repent their ways, God may cut them down like tall trees. The power of monarch and the fate of a nation are in the hand of the Almighty God. Doing God's will and obeying God's law lengthen the prosperity of a nation.

Table 5. Daniel's interpretation of Belshazzar's vision of the handwriting on the wall

The Vision	Interpretation	Warning to the king	Fulfillment of the Vision
Fingers of a human hand appeared and wrote on the plaster of the wall saying, *Mene, Mene, Tarkel, Parsin* [NIV Study Bible (Fully Revised), p.1328]	*"Mene*: God has numbered the days of your reign and brought it to an end." (Da. 5:26) *"Tarkel*: You have been weighed on the scale and found wanting." (Da. 5:27) *"Peres*: Your kingdom is divided and given to the Medes and Persians." (Da. 5:28)	You…have not humbled yourself, though you knew all this (his father Nebuchadnezzar's mental illness). Instead, you have set yourself up against the Lord of heaven. (Da. 5:22-23).	Belshazzar was slain that very night and Darius, the Medes, at age 62, took over the kingdom. (*Gubaru* may be another name for Darius the Medes that King Cyrus put in charge of the newly conquered Babylonia territories. (NIV footnote 5:31, p.1328).

Source. *Adapted from* Zondervan NIV Study Bible (Fully Revised) and Study notes. Copyright© 1985, 1995, 2002 by Zondervan), 1327-1328.

Chapter 5. KEY POINTS

1. By defiling holy items brought from Jerusalem, drank from them, and while drinking, praised idol gods, Belshazzar and his cohort blasphemed the Lord. God conveyed His judgment through a hand-written message on the wall that predicted the demise of the Babylonian Empire.

2. Daniel told Belshazzar that despite his knowledge of his predecessor's arrogance and unrepentant heart that resulted in a mental illness, he failed to learn the lesson of humility from Nebuchadnezzar's experience. He knowingly sinned against Jehovah. The night, after Daniel interpreted the writings to him, Belshazzar was assassinated, and Darius the Medes of the Persian Empire took over Babylon.

3. Daniel's psychospiritual power was revealed in his ability to decipher the hand-written message on the wall that predicted the demise of the Babylonian empire and his boldness in delivering the fateful message to Belshazzar.

4. God affirmed the virtues of humility, justice, and righteousness.

CHAPTER 6

To Pray Or Not To Pray When Life Is Threatened:
Daniel In The Lions' Den –
The Severest Test Of Daniel's Psychospirituality

My God sent his angel, and he shut the mouth
of the lion. They have not hurt me, because I was
found innocent in his sight (Daniel 6:22)

A t late life, Daniel faced the severest test of his psychospirituality while serving his new boss, Persian King Cyrus (circa 539 B.C.) (See table 1). In chapter 3, you have noted how Daniel's friends were the subjects of a plot to destroy them. Now it was Daniel's turn. His enemies hatched a scheme to kill him. Will Daniel prevail?

During King Cyrus's reign, Daniel's exceptional abilities so distinguished himself among the administrators and satraps that the king planned to promote him to oversee the whole kingdom. As a Chinese saying goes, "The tall tree invites wind." Indeed, Daniel was about to become the tallest tree in Persia. This imminent promotion provoked the jealousy of all the Persian administrators and satraps, and they schemed to destroy him. Unable to find any ground to bring charges against Daniel, the schemers knew that the only way to have a basis of charges must be something that had to do with the law of his God, his beliefs, and his faith.

So the group convinced the king to issue a decree that for the next thirty days, anyone who prayed to any god or man and not the king shall be thrown into the lions' den. Like many monarchs before him, King Cyrus easily succumbed to the temptation of flattery and pride!

When Daniel learned about the decree, he faced the choice of obeying the king's edict or to continue to pray to his God. Daniel chose to adhere to his faith, and continued his usual habit of praying three times a day in his upstairs' room, facing Jerusalem. His enemies reported Daniel's defiance to the king. When the king heard this, he was greatly distressed. He suddenly realized that he had been tricked. Because of his fondness and respect for Daniel, the king made every effort that day to save him. But it was of no avail. The king must carry out his own decree.

So Daniel was thrown into the lions' den. That night, the king couldn't sleep. At the first light of dawn, the king hurried to the lions' den and called to Daniel in an anguished voice, "Daniel, servant of the living God, has your God, whom you serve continually, been able to rescue you from the lions?" (Daniel 6:20) Daniel answered that he was unharmed, as his God had sent an angel to shut the mouth of the lions. Furthermore, he proclaimed his innocence before the king (Daniel 6:22).

The king was overjoyed and ordered Daniel be lifted out of the den. And to Daniel's enemies, those who had falsely brought the charges against Daniel, along with their wives and children, he commanded all be thrown into the lions' den.

The king then wrote a decree praising the God of Daniel, saying:
    For he is a living God
    and he endures forever;
    his kingdom will not be destroyed,
    his dominion will never end (Daniel 6:26).

So the honor of the Jewish God bestowed during the Babylonian reign was now also institutionalized in Persia. The Persian king bowed down to the King of kings because of Daniel's steadfast faith in his God. God, in turn, protected and saved Daniel.

This episode reveals Daniel's impeccable character: no hint of pride, greed, or any misconduct in his loyal service to his king. Facing the threat of death, Daniel did not compromise his faith and continued praying to his God. When rescued, Daniel knew how to affirm his faith in God and his loyalty to the king. The man of God had so conducted himself that the gentile king loved and respected him. As a result, Jehovah's name was honored and His might reaffirmed in the new empire. Daniel made it happened. Such was Daniel, the man.

Chapter 6. KEY POINTS

1. Daniel faced the severest test of his spirituality late in life when he defied the Persian king's order by not praying to him.

2. Daniel was thrown into the lions' den for his defiance, but God rescued him.

3. The King was so thrilled that Daniel was found alive. Through Daniel's uncompromising faith, the Persian king acknowledged the supremacy of the living God.

4. Daniel's psychospirituality prevailed against his enemies because of his unshakable faith in the living God, his impeccable service to the king, and his incorrigible character.

PART 2

Daniel's Dream and Visions:

The Subjective Manifestation of Daniel's Psychospirituality

CHAPTER 7

Dream And Vision Of
The Four Beasts

But the saints of the Most High will receive the kingdom and will possess it forever–yes, for ever [sic] and ever (Daniel 7:18)

C hapter 7 is an important transitional chapter. There are three thematic threads: 1) A connection with Nebuchadnezzar's dream in chapter 2, but expanded in scope to focus on trial for God's people; 2) A panoramic view of world history that began from the Babylonian period extending to the end of time; and 3) God's eventual triumph and the establishment of a kingdom to be ruled by the "son of man."

This chapter reveals the dream and vision of the four beasts that Daniel had during the first year of Belshazzar's reign (circa 553-539 B.C.), around 553 B.C. This vision preceded Belshazzar's vision of "handwriting on the wall" elaborated in chapter 5.

Daniel wrote down the vision of the four beasts after he dreamed. The vision passed through his mind while lying on his bed. In a moment of solitude, in what appeared to be a hypnagogic experience, a twilight stage of consciousness between wakefulness and asleep, Daniel received this revelation from God. With our present knowledge of the brain, the dream suggested that God conveyed His message to the deep unconscious stratum of Daniel's brain where dreams supposedly originated (See chapter 14, on Dreams). As the dream passed through Daniel's higher center brain, the cortical area that is responsible for conscious thought and analysis became actively engaged so that the haziness of the dream evolved into clear visions. Daniel quickly wrote these down before the content of the dream and vision began to fade, as dreams tended to happen. Thus, Daniel preserved for posterity the importance and significance of these visions.

Daniel's vision unfolded in the following sequence:
1.   First, he saw four winds of heaven churning up the great sea (Daniel 7:20).

2.   Then, four beasts, each different from the others, came up out of the sea (Daniel 7:3).

3.   Finally, the Ancient of Days [presumably God] appeared. Then one that is like a "son of man", coming with the clouds of heaven, approached the Ancient of Days, and was led into His presence. He was given authority, glory and sovereign power; all nations and people worshipped him; and his dominion lasted forever (Daniel 7:9, 13-14).

The four great beasts were thought to symbolize the following empires:
1.   The lion with wings of an eagle, the kingdom of Babylonia.

2.   The bear that had three ribs in its mouth, Medo-Persia.

3.   The leopard that had four heads and four wings, Greece.

4.   The "terrifying, frightening and powerful kingdom", a fourth unidentified kingdom.[10] (See table 6).

These four empires will rise from the earth, but eventually God's eternal kingdom will replace them.

Daniel was particularly interested in the meaning of the fourth beast, which was different from all the other. This beast was most terrifying, with its iron teeth and bronze claws that "crushed and devoured its victims and trampled underfoot whatever was left" (Daniel 7:19). Then a "little horn" which had "eyes of a man and a mouth that spoke boastfully" came up from them. This horn will speak against the Most High, wage war against the saints and defeat them until the Ancient of Days came and pronounced judgment in favor of the saints of the Most High and the time came when they possessed the kingdom (Daniel 7:21-22).

Conservative biblical commentators have attributed the fourth beast to a future Roman world power, the antichrist, near the end time.[11] [There are two "little horns" mentioned in Daniel (one in chapter 7 and the other in chapter 8), the "little horn" of chapter 7 was thought to represent the antichrist].[12]

The vision deeply troubled Daniel and he couldn't understand it. He was shaken up, his face turned pale caused by fear and strong sympathetic nervous system discharge that shook his body. What possibly was troubling Daniel? Was it because he couldn't understand the meaning of the vision? Were the images of the struggle near the end time too traumatic? Could Daniel be frightened, as the prophets Isaiah (6:5), Jeremiah (4:19), Ezekiel (1:28; 3:15) and the apostle John in Revelation (1:17) were, when they caught a glimpse of the image of God Almighty? Could Daniel knew too much the secrets of the world to come, including the revelation of the fate of the kings and nations he was serving, yet, he was not in a position to tell the king or anyone else? Or, could it be a combination of all these factors and more. We do not know and are left to speculate. It is certainly within reason that men, even holy man like Daniel, when they caught glimpses of the holy rays of God, their sinful nature would be exposed. The prophet Isaiah had this experience when he cried out, "Woe to me! I am ruined! For I am a man of unclean lips and I live among men of unclean lips, and my eyes have seen the King, the Lord Almighty" (Isaiah 6:5).

Daniel was helpless. He couldn't understand the dream and had to rely on the one standing there [angel] to explain its meaning. Put in a position in which God was directly revealing messages to him, all earthly knowledge and training Daniel had acquired as a diviner of dreams were useless. It was as if God wanted Daniel to realize that he must be humble, completely discard his own intelligence, ability, and pre-conception, and became an "empty vessel" so that God's messages can fill him.

In this chapter, Daniel saw the transience, vulnerabilities, ugliness, sinfulness of human nature, and the follies of human enterprises. He saw the devastation wrought about at end time by antichrist symbolized by the "terrifying, frightening and powerful beast." He witnessed the eventual destruction of the beast. He caught a glimpse of the glory of God and the second coming of the Messiah. Daniel saw the panorama of the human history, its end and the world to come afterward. These experiences overwhelmed him. He knew too much, but had to carry the burden of that knowledge all by himself. Yet, he complied and willingly submitted to God's will at great personal emotional cost. God occupied first place in Daniel's heart. Because he was a willing "vessel", God revealed to him the secrets of the future.

Table 6. Daniel's dream and vision of the four beasts

The Dream and Vision (Scriptural Verses)	Interpretation	Warning	Fulfillment of the Vision
Four winds of heaven churning up the great sea. Four great beasts, each different from the others, came up out of the sea and they looked like:	Four beasts-- four kingdoms that will rise from the earth.	Four empires will come and greatly affect Israel.	Appearance of the four kingdoms of Neo-Babylon (626 B.C.), Medo-Persia (539 B.C.), Greece (330 B.C.), and Rome (63 B.C.)
1st, a lion had wings of an n eagle. Its wings were torn off and it was lifted from the ground so that it stood on two feet like a man, and the heart of a man was given to it.	*The Lion*--Neo-Babylonian Empire. The rest perhaps reflects the humbling of Nebuchadnezzar. (NIV study note: 7:4-7)	The humbling of the monarch	Neo-Babylon Empire
2nd, a bear, "it was raised up on one of its each sides, and it had three ribs in its mouth between its teeth. It was told, 'Get up and eat your fill of flesh!'"	*The bear*--"refers to the superior status of the Persians in the Medo-Persian Alliance." Three ribs— may represent three principal conquests.		Medo-Persia and her conquest of: • Lydia (546 B.C.), • Babylon (539 B.C.), • Egypt (525 B.C.)

3rd, a leopard had 4 wings on its back like those of a bird. The beast had four heads, and it was given authority to rule.	*The leopard*: represents the speedy conquest of Alexander the Great (334-330). Four heads—four main divisions into which his empire fell after his untimely death.	Fast conquest by Greece	Greece under Alexander the Great (334-330 B.C.) The four empires under Alexander's general: • Macedon and Greece (under Antipater and Cassander), • Thrace and Asian Minor (under Lysimachus), • Syria (under Seleucus I), • The Holy Land and Egypt (under Ptolemy I)
4th, a terrifying, frightening and powerful beast had ten horns with large iron teeth. It crushed and devoured its victims and trampled underfoot whatever was left.	*The terrifying beast*: the Roman Empire. Ten horns as in the "ten toes in Nebuchadnezzar statue."	Conquest by Rome, and later, devastation by the Roman emperors	Past and future Roman Empire

	Ten teeth: "a later configuration of states occupying the territories formerly controlled by the Roman Empire." (NIV study note: 2:32-43)		
Another horn, a little one, which came up among them; three of the first horns were uprooted before it. The horn had eyes like the eyes of a man and a mouth that spoke boastfully.	Another horn— the antichrist or a world power sharing the characteristics of the antichrist (NIV note: 7:8)	Appearance of a ruler who will cause great devastation to God's people	Appearance of the antichrist
"Thrones were set in place, and the Ancient of Days took his seat. His clothing was as white as snow; the hair of its head was white as wool. His throne was flaming with fire, and its wheels were all ablaze. A river of fire was flowing,	Ancient of Days—God. A description of the majesty and splendor of God.	God will appear.	Future appearance of God

coming out from before him. Thousands upon thousands attended him; ten thousand times ten thousand stood before him. The court was seated, and the books were opened."			
The horn which was speaking with the boastful words was slain. Its body destroyed and was thrown into the blazing fire. "(The other beasts had been stripped of their authority, but were allowed to live for a period of time.)"	The horn -- the antichrist or a world power sharing in the characteristics of the antichrist will be destroyed forever." (NIV notes 7:8, p.1331)	The antichrist will be destroyed.	Future destruction of the antichrist
A son of man coming with the clouds of heaven, approached the Ancient of Days and was led into his presence. He was given authority, glory and sovereign power.	Son of Man— First reference to the Messiah as Son of Man. Jesus applied the title to himself. The sovereignty, power and greatness of the kingdoms	The Messiah will come again.	Second coming of Christ and the establishment of an everlasting kingdom

All peoples, nations and men of every language worshipped him. His dominion is an everlasting dominion that will not pass away and his kingdom is one that will never be destroyed.	under the whole heavens will be handed over to the saints, the people of the most high. His kingdom will rule forever. (NIV Study note, p. 1331)		

Source. *Adapted from* Zondervan NIV Study Bible (Fully Revised), Copyright© 1985, 1995, 2002 by Zondervan), 1330-1332.

Chapter 7. KEY POINTS

1. Daniel dreamed and had a vision of four beasts that foretold the world to come.

2. This vision portrayed a panoramic view of world's history, starting from the Babylonian empire and lasting till the end of time, with the appearance of the "son of man" who will establish God's eternal kingdom on earth.

3. The symbolism of the four beasts was thought to represent the succession of four empires: Babylon, Medo-Persia, Greece, and Rome.

4. Daniel was particularly interested in the meaning of "little horn" that grew out of the terrifying "fourth beast." Many biblical scholars considered the "little horn" to represent the antichrist which will appear during the end time of the world.

5. At end time, one like the "son of man" will come with the clouds of heaven and will approach the Ancient of Days and be led into God's presence. He will be given authority, glory, and sovereign power. All nations and people will worship him and his dominion will last forever. This "son of man" has been interpreted to be the Messiah.

6. The vision deeply troubled Daniel. He couldn't interpret the vision and had to rely on an angel for interpretation.

7. Daniel's psychospirituality enabled him to receive the first of a series of visions from God. It empowered him to see the future. But in doing so, he had to pay an enormous emotional price as he became totally helpless and fearful in the presence of the Lord Almighty. Understanding how Daniel worked through this paradox and persistently pursued God's will, would reveal Daniel's character and psychospirituality.

CHAPTER 8

Vision Of The Ram And The Goat

The vision of the evenings and mornings that has
been given you is true, but seal up the vision, for
it concerns the distant future (Daniel 8:26)

I n the third year of King Belshazzar reign (circa 551 B.C.), Daniel
received his second vision. Daniel saw himself in the citadel of
Susa, in the province of Elam [now part of modern Iraq], beside
the Ulai Canal. In this vision, Daniel saw a goat with a prominent
horn between his eyes that came from the west, charged furiously
against a two-horned ram and trampled him on the ground. The
goat became very great, but at the height of his power his large horn
was broken off. In its place, four prominent horns grew up towards
the four winds of heaven.

Then another horn that came out of them which started small,
grew in power to the south and to the east and toward the Beautiful
Land until it reached the host of the heavens, threw some of the starry
host down to the earth, and trampled on them. (Daniel 8:9-10) This
little horn set itself up to be as great as the Prince of the host, took
away the daily sacrifice from him, and brought low the place of his
sanctuary. "Because of the rebellion, the host of the saints, and the

daily sacrifice were given to it. It prospered in everything it did, and truth was thrown to the ground" (Daniel 8:9-12).

A conversation ensued between two holy men concerning how long will it take for the vision to be fulfilled. One holy one said to Daniel, "…2,300 evenings and mornings; then the sanctuary will be re-consecrated" (Daniel 8:13-14).

Then, the angel Gabriel gave the interpretation of the vision. The shaggy goat was the king of Greece, Alexander the Great (Daniel 8:21). The two-horned ram represented the kings of Media and Persia (Daniel 8:20). This vision depicted how Alexander the Great swiftly defeated the kings of Media and Persia. But at the height of his power, Alexander died [in 323 B.C.]. After his death, his empire was divided into four among his generals. Then a stern face-faced king [Antiochus Epiphanes IV], symbolized by the "small horn", rose to power by intrigue and deceit. He caused astounding devastation and destroyed the "mighty men and holy people." He set himself equal to God. But in the end God destroyed him (table 7).

Concerning the meaning of "2,300 evenings and mornings" for the fulfillment of this vision, it probably referred to the number of sacrifices consecutively offered on 1,150 days [1,150 x 2, for two daily sacrifices for the continual burnt offering], and was the interval between the desecration of the Lord's altar by Antiochus Epiphanes IV and its re-consecration by Judas Maccabeus on Kislev 25, 165 B.C. (NIV note 8:14, p. 1333).

This was a frightening vision. It left Daniel totally exhausted. It evoked in him the most intense emotional reaction so far and he became ill for several days. The severity of his emotional reaction suggested the seriousness of the forthcoming events with deep implications for the Jewish people. It also predicted the desecration of God's temple. When Daniel recovered, he went about doing the king's business. But he was appalled by the vision. He was almost in a hazy state of mind. He couldn't understand it and he kept the vision to himself.

What this vision unfolded for Daniel was the fate of Israel under the Medo-Persian and Grecian empires. A series of events culminated in the desecration of the temple under Antiochus IV Epiphanes. This devastation involved his people and their temple. The experience was too painful and traumatic, and left Daniel's mind and brain feeling hazy. The depth of his emotional response revealed how much Daniel cared for and loved his people.

Again, Daniel's emotional reaction to this vision (See table 10) was totally different from the fortitude behavior he displayed when he was interpreting dreams and visions to the Babylonian kings. With the kings, Daniel was confident, erudite, and assertive. In this vision, he was helpless, exhausted, and became ill. He was appalled and befuddled. Why was there such a contrast in Daniel's behavior? Didn't he still retain the ability to divine and interpret dream and vision? After all, this vision occurred during Belshazzar's reign while he was at the prime of his career and possessing the power of divination. Was there a hidden spiritual message?

As in chapter 7, we can only speculate. Since this vision occurred during Belshazzar's reign, Daniel was given an apocalyptic revelation of the fate of the Babylonian and Persian king and empire. History tells us that Alexander defeated Persian King Darius in the final and decisive Battle of Gaugamela, near the town of Arbela at 331 B.C. Darius fled to the northern province but was murdered by one of his officers. Alexander then assumed the title of King of Persia. The bloodshed caused by the battles between Alexander and Darius was troublesome enough. But the climax of the insult was the desecration of the Lord's altar under Antiochus IV. Being a devoted Jew, this probably horrified Daniel. It was an act so appalling that defied imagination. For Daniel to go through this traumatic experience, it must have been extremely terrifying and sad. He literally became sick (Daniel 8:27).

Daniel's emotional reaction in chapter 8 seemed to share similar meaning to his reaction in chapter 7. Chapter 8 conveyed the impression that there was a limit to human intelligence, understanding, and emotional endurance when the Almighty God revealed his vision and apocalyptical events to his servants. In chapter 1, you saw how God honored and gave Daniel human intelligence and the ability to interpret dreams and visions. However, in chapter 8, Daniel was deprived of that divining power; his emotional reaction was simply like that of a common man. This suggested that God chooses the person, at His own time, to become an empty vessel to receive His vision. It is the prerogative for the Almighty to give or to take away. You can discern Daniel's physical and emotional make-up was not much different from other mortals. But his spiritual qualities and character endeared him to God. His psychospirituality was the main reason God chose him to be the conduit of the revelation of His will and visions to both His chosen people and to the gentiles. Even though Daniel's felt devastated, they were short-lived. God fixed a definite period in which His suffering people can expect deliverance. And that conveyed hope.

Table 7. Daniel's vision of a ram and a goat

Vision (Scriptural Verses)	Interpretation	Fulfillment of the Vision
Daniel saw himself in the citadel of Susa in the province of Elam, beside the Ulai Canal. A ram with two long horns was standing before Daniel.	Two horn rams---kings of Media and Persia	Media and Persia
One horn was longer but grew up later. The ram charged towards the west, the north and the south. No animal could stand against him, and none	One horn – one of the Persian kings.	Persia

could rescue from his power. He became great and can do as he pleased.

Suddenly, a goat with a prominent horn between his eyes came from the west, crossing the whole earth without touching the ground. He charged against and attacked the ram with great rage, shattering his two horns. The goat knocked the ram to the ground and trampled on him, and none could rescue the ram from his power. The goat became very great, but at the height of his power his large horn was broken off. In its place, four prominent horns grew up toward the four winds of heaven.	Shaggy goat is Alexander. He attacked Persia. The four horns that replaced the one that was broken off refer to the four kingdoms that will emerge from his nation but will not have the same power.	Greece under Alexander the Great (334-330 B.C.). The four empires under Alexander's general: • Macedon and Greece (under Antipater and Cassander), • Thrace and Asian Minor (under Lysimachus) • Syria (under Seleucus I) • The Holy Land and Egypt (under Ptolemy I) (NIV Study notes 7:4-7, p. 1331)
Out of one of them became another horn, which started small but grew in power to the south and to the east and toward the Beautiful Land. It grew until it reached the host of heavens and it threw down	Another king arose not from the ten horns belonging to the fourth kingdom (as in 7:8), but rather from one of the four horns belonging to the third kingdom	Antiochus IV Epiphanes caused astounding devastation and succeeded in whatever he does. He destroyed the mighty men and holy people. He caused deceit to proper, and he considered

some of the starry host down to the earth and trampled on them. It set itself up as the Prince of the host; it took away the daily sacrifices from him, and the place of his sanctuary was brought low. It prospered in everything it did, and truth was thrown to the ground.	refers to Antiochus IV.	himself superior. He took his stand against the Prince of princes. Antiochus died in 164 B.C. at Tabae in Persia.
Then Daniel heard a holy one speaking, and another holy one said to him, "How long will it take for the vision to be fulfilled---the vision concerning the daily sacrifice, the rebellion that causes desolation, and the surrender of the sanctuary and of the host that will be trampled underfoot?" He said to Daniel, "It will take 2,300 evenings and mornings; then the sanctuary will be re-consecrated."	"2,300 evenings and mornings" probably "refer to the number of sacrifices consecutively offered on 1,150 days, the interval between the desecration of the Lord's altar by Antiochus Epiphanes and its re-consecration by Judas Maccabeus on Kislev 25, 165 B.C." (NIV Study Notes 8:14, p. 1333)	Judas Maccabeus

Source. *Adapted from* Zondervan NIV Study Bible (Fully Revised), Copyright© 1985, 1995, 2002. 1332-1333.

Chapter 8. KEY POINTS

1. Daniel's second vision of a Ram and a Goat occurred during Belshazzar's reign.

2. The Goat with a prominent horn symbolized Alexander the Great of Greece. The two-horned Ram, the king of Media and Persia.

3. Alexander the Great swiftly conquered Medo-Persia. But he died at the height of his career, leaving his vast empire divided among his four generals.

4. A "little horn" identified by biblical commentators as Antiochus Epiphanes IV arose. He set himself equal to God, caused astounding devastation, and destroyed the mighty men and holy people.

5. The vision predicted an interval of 1,150 days representing the period between the desecration of the Lord's altar by Antiochus Epiphanes IV, and its restoration by Judas Maccabeus in 165 B.C.

6. Daniel was frightened, exhausted, and became ill for several days. The vision evoked in him the most intense emotional reaction so far.

7. Daniel's psychospirituality was again revealed in his willingness to accept the conveyance of God's vision, despite the emotional toll it exacted on him.

CHAPTER 9

Prayer For Israel And The Restoration Of Jerusalem

O Lord, listen! O Lord, forgive! O Lord, hear and act!
For your sake, O my God, do not delay, because your
city and your people bear your name (Daniel 9:19)

T his chapter consists of Daniel's petition to God for the restoration of Judah and reconstruction of Jerusalem, and God's
response. It was written as hard facts of history, a narrative
style that is a departure from all the other chapters. The events narrated were a crucial turning point in the Jewish history that may be
as significant as the founding of the modern State of Israel in 1948.
It conveyed an acute sense of historical moment. Daniel was acting
like the high priest petitioning for his people. He was once more the
active, assertive, and erudite person he was known for. In response,
God gave Daniel a message and a vision.

The narrative stated that during the first year of King Cyrus
(Darius, the Medes)[13] reign (539 B.C.), Daniel, by now more than
eighty years old, having read the prophet Jeremiah's prophecy that
the desolation of Jerusalem would last seventy years, realized that
the time for the Jewish exiles to return to rebuild Jerusalem had

arrived. He passionately pleaded with God for forgiveness on behalf of his people and to end the desolation of Jerusalem (Daniel 9:1-19). Daniel's prayer summed up the transgressions and sin of his people and the disgrace to Jehovah's name. It was time to act. Daniel pleaded with to God to show mercy. Listen to his passionate petition.

> Now, our God, hear our prayers and petitions of your servant. For your sake, O Lord. Look with favor on your desolate sanctuary. Give ear, O Lord, and hear, open your eyes and see the desolation of the city that bears your Name. We do not make request of you because we are righteous, but because of your great mercy. O Lord, listen! O Lord forgive! O Lord, hear and act! For your sake, O my God, do not delay, because your city and your people bear your name. (Daniel 9:17-19)

Then in chapter 1:1 of the book of Ezra, King Cyrus of Persia made this surprising proclamation.

> In the first year of Cyrus king of Persia, in order to fulfill the word of the Lord spoken by Jeremiah, the Lord moved the heart of Cyrus king of Persia to make a proclamation throughout his realm and to put in writing…The Lord, the Lord of heaven, has given me all the kingdoms of the earth and he has appointed me to build a temple for him at Jerusalem in Judah. (Ezra 1-2)

This was an unprecedented generous and gracious act of a gentile monarch that fulfilled Jeremiah's prophecy. Who moved the heart of the Lord? In turn, moved the heart of Cyrus? The Bible was silent regarding Daniel's role in the king's decision. Daniel's prayer preceded Cyrus's decree to allow the first batch of Jewish exiles led by Zerubbabel to return to Palestine (Ezra 2:2; Nehemiah 7:7). But judging from Daniel's previous behavior when he served under Nebuchadnezzar and Belshazzar, it is very reasonable to infer that Daniel must have influenced the king's decision. Daniel had waited long for this moment to come, and he sure wasn't going to let the opportunity passed by without acting.

God answered Daniel's petition by sending the angel Gabriel who declared.

> Daniel, I have now come to give you insight and understanding. As soon as you began to pray, an answer was given, which I have come to tell you, for you are highly esteemed. Therefore consider the message and understand the vision:

> Seventy sevens are decreed for your people and your holy city to finish transgression, to put an end to sin, to atone for wickedness, to bring in everlasting righteousness, to seal up vision and prophecy and to anoint the most holy.

> Know and understand this: From the time of the decree to restore and rebuild Jerusalem until the Anointed One, the ruler, comes, there will be seventy 'sevens,' and sixty-two 'sevens.' It will be rebuilt with streets and a trench, but in times of trouble. After the sixty-two 'sevens,' the Anointed One will be cut off and will have nothing. The people of the ruler will come will destroy the city and the sanctuary. The end will come like a flood: War will continue until the end, and desolations have been decreed. He will confirm a covenant with many for one 'seven.' In the middle of the 'seven' he will put an end to sacrifice and offering. And on a wing of the temple, he will set up an abomination that causes destruction, until the end that is decreed is poured out on him. (Daniel 9:22-27)

The message contained 6 purposes for the people of God to fulfill:

1. To finish transgression;
2. To put an end to sin;
3. To atone for wickedness;
4. To bring in everlasting righteousness;
5. To seal up vision and prophecy; and
6. To anoint the most holy. (Daniel 9:24)

NIV Study notes commented that all the above six purposes were to be fulfilled through the Messiah. Some believed that the last three were not yet achieved by the time of Christ's crucifixion and resurrection but awaits his future action.[14]

As for the vision of the seventy 'sevens', the NIV Study Notes explained it this way (p.1335):

1. Each "seven" represents 7 years. Thus, seventy "7" would be 490 years [70 x 7 =490].

2. The 490 years is divided into two critical periods: an early "483" and a late "7" years.

   a. The period of 483 years is further divided into 2 periods: A seven "7s" (49 years) and a sixty-two "7s" (434 years). [(7 x7) + (7 x 62) = 49 + 434 = 483].

      • Four hundred thirty four years [62 x 7 = 434, sixty two "7s"] was the interval between the time of authorizing the rebuilding of Jerusalem [Ezra 7:1] until the coming of the Messiah; and,

      • Forty nine years [7 x 7 = 49, seven "7s"] was the period from the crucifixion of the Messiah until the destruction of Jerusalem by the Roman Emperor Titus in 70 A.D. (Daniel 9:26).

   b. A final "seven" years referred to an event at the end time. It foretold the appearance of another "little horn" or antichrist who will set up "the abomination that causes desolation". "He will confirm a covenant with many for one '7.' In the middle of the '7' he will put an end to sacrifice and offering. And on a wing of the temple, he will set up an abomination that causes desolation, until the end that is decreed is poured out on him." (Daniel 9:27) Biblical scholars referred this vivid and remarkable event to an indeterminate period in the future in which the antichrist will conclude a peace treaty with Israel, but then break off the pact after three and a half years.[15]

The chapter ended with this incredible message and vision!

Daniel's response to Jeremiah's prophecy showed how informed he was about the scripture. His understanding of Jewish history defined his role and gave him a keen appreciation of the emotional and spiritual needs of his people. He realized the accumulation of the weight of sin and transgressions that caused the Jewish Diaspora. He couldn't bear any second longer to witness their suffering and shame. His heart bled for them. It was time to restore God's temple and honor. He acted by assuming leadership and passionately prayed.

What a mensch![16] Even though he had talents, wisdom and knowledge, his character exuded humility, confidence, assertiveness and spirituality. His close relation with God was likened to two intimate friends. In a cause he believed in and in accordance with God's will, he did not hesitate to pull God's heart cords (See also chapter 17). And how the Lord loved, esteemed, and responded to him! Before he finished his prayer and petition, God had already answered.

The experience of Daniel shows you how God can use an intelligent, spiritual, humble, and action-oriented man to reveal and accomplish His will. God revealed to Daniel and acted through him to restore the Jewish nation and His temple in Jerusalem.

Chapter 9. KEY POINTS

1. Daniel received his third vision during Persian King Cyrus's reign.

2. Daniel realized that according to the prophet Jeremiah's prophecy, seventy years of desolation had passed. It was time for the Jewish people to return to Judah and restore Jerusalem. Daniel then fervently prayed and petitioned Jehovah for this to happen.

3. The swiftness [before he concluded his prayer] of God's response to his prayer indicates how God esteemed and loved Daniel. The angel Gabriel conveyed to him a message and the vision of the "seventy '7s'."

4. The vision of the "seventy '7s'" provided a time line of the tasks God's people to fulfill in order to bring about everlasting righteousness.

5. Daniel's psychospiritual power was revealed in how he petitioned God and by the swiftness God answered his prayer.

CHAPTER 10

Vision Of A Man Dressed In Linen

Do not be afraid, Daniel. Since the first day that you
set your mind to gain understanding and to humble
yourself before your God, your words were heard, and
I have come in response to them (Daniel 10:12)

C hapter 10 documents Daniel's fourth vision about a "man dressed in linen" during the third year of Persian King Cyrus's reign (537 B.C.), his emotional reaction, and the message concerning a great war that would greatly affect his people. The whole chapter was almost devoted to a description of Daniel's psychological reaction to the vision, and his interaction with an angel before the details of the vision were revealed in chapters 11-12 (See table 8).

We were told that Daniel mourned [fasted] for three weeks. Despite his previous emotional response that sapped his energy and vitality when he received God's vision (See table 10), Daniel again was actively seeking God's revelations. After his fast, as he was standing on the bank of the Tigris River, Daniel saw a "man dressed in linen" with incredible splendors (Daniel 10:5). The vision terrified Daniel that left him totally weak. His face turned deathly pale. He fell into a deep sleep [trance] with his face to the ground (Daniel 10:8). During this totally helpless state, the hand of an angel touched and set him trembling on his hands and knees. Then, the angel conveyed a most reassuring and testimonial message to him:

> Daniel, you who are highly esteemed...do not be afraid. Since the first day that you set your mind to gain understanding and to humble yourself before your God, your words were heard, and I have come in response to them (Daniel 10:11-12).

Here the angel revealed the key to Daniel's psychospirituality: Daniel sets his mind to *gain* understanding and to *humble* himself before God. This willful choice and attitude set him apart from other mortals. As you traced his life's activities--from his early refusal to eat ceremonially-unclean food, to seeking God's will through dream and vision and subjecting himself to the emotional strain that accompanied these experiences--Daniel's *determination* in seeking God's will stood out. And now, the angel affirmed Daniel's psychospirituality. The angel's statement testified to a maturing relationship between Daniel and God. The transcendental experience reminded him to put his total reliance on God and this served as a bulwark against all external temptations, assaults, and pride. This message was conveyed particularly through his repeated experience of "helplessness" even as Daniel continually sought God's revelations. It was as if God kept reminding him...Daniel, remember, you are a mortal whom I am using. Be humble. Do not be afraid. Be strong.

Daniel's determination to know Jehovah is a shining example to all who wish to seek a closer relationship with God. God chooses to reveal through dream and vision to a willing mind. The combination of a willing mind to know God and humility to serve was a key foundation of Daniel's psychospiritual power. (See also chapter 17 on the Power of Humility)

Table 8. Daniel's emotional reactions to his visions

Visions	Daniel's Emotional Reaction	Interpretation
The vision of the Beasts and the Son of Man (Ch. 7)	"As for me Daniel, my spirit was anxious on account of this, while the visions of my head were troubling me." (7:15) NIV	"The emphasis on the first person… marks the break in the vision when the seer comes to himself. The verb rendered 'was anxious'… has the sense of being 'short' in spirit, and means constraint, impatience, anxiety, and the like. This oppression is the motive which makes the seer bold to accost one of 'the assistants…On the other hand, Rev.5:4, sometimes adduced as a parallel, implies grief."[1]
	"This is the end of the matter. I, Daniel, was deeply troubled by my thoughts, and my face turned pale, but I kept the matter to myself." (7:28)	"*I Daniel – much were my thoughts troubling me*: The seer is recalled to himself, as in (7:15); the phrase, describing his affection of the mind, appears above (5:6,10). *And my color changed* [for the phrases. at (5:6,9,10)], *and the matter* [a potential *word*] *I kept in my heart*. The literary composition of the vision was later, as indeed was the case with the oracles of the great Prophets; a book was finally compiled and concluded, (12:4)] "[1]

The vision of the Ram and goat (Ch. 8)	"I, Daniel, was exhausted and lay ill for several days. Then I got up and went about the king's business. I was appalled by the vision: it was beyond under-standing. (8:27)	"Daniel was befallen with a stroke of illness. *And I was appalled (perplexed)* (See also the phrase 'I heard and could not understand' [12:8] serves as introduction to the following chapter in which the seer agonizes for further illumination."[1]
A Man dressed in linen (Ch. 10)	At that time, Daniel mourned for three weeks, ate no choice food, meat or wine, and used no lotions (10:2)	Daniel fasted in order to receive the vision.
	On the 24th day after he saw the vision, Daniel had no strength left, his face turned deathly pale, and he was helpless. As he heard the man spoke, he fell into a deep sleep, his face to the ground. A hand touched him and set him trembling on his hands and knees. When told to stand up and listen, Daniel stood up trembling (10:7-11).	"The phrase (the conclu-sion) 'signifies the closing stage' of the present trial."[2]

	When told about what will happen to his people concerning a time yet to come, Daniel bowed with his face toward the ground and was speechless. He began to speak only when the one who was standing before him touched his lips. Daniel said he was overcome with anguish because of the vision, and he was helpless. His strength was gone and he could hardly breathe. Again, the one who looked like a man touched him and gave him strength (10:15-19).	
The end time (Ch. 12)	I heard, but I did not understand (12:8).	Daniel was perplexed by the vision and he did not get the answer to his request to know the end time.

Source. *Adapted from* Zondervan NIV Study Bible (Fully Revised), pp.1330-1340.

---

[1] James A. Montgomery, A Critical and Exegetical Commentary on the Book of Daniel. The International Commentary, (Edinburgh: T. and T. Clark, 1964).

[2] Ibid., 476-477.

Chapter 10. KEY POINTS

1. Daniel fasted and actively sought for and received his fourth vision during the 3rd year of King Cyrus's reign.

2. The vision was about a "man dressed in linen" and the message concerning a great war that will affect the Israelites.

3. Daniel felt helpless, speechless, breathless, and weak in response to the vision. But the man dressed in linen touched, strengthened, praised, reassured, and encouraged him.

4. The testimony of the angel revealed a key element of Daniel's psychospirituality: his determination to gain understanding of God's will and his humility before God.

CHAPTER 11

The Kings Of The South And The North

Some of the wise will stumble, so that they may be refined, purified and made spotless until the time of the end…(Daniel 11:35)

The angel now revealed to Daniel details of the "great war" mentioned in chapter 10. Alexander the Great defeated Persia. After his untimely death in 323 B.C., Alexander's empire was divided among his four generals. A series of wars in the struggle for supremacy ensued. (See table 9) The wars waged between the kings of the South (the Ptolemy's) and the North (the Seleucids) was particularly significant to Israel. Israel, the Beautiful Land, will succumb to the invader from the North, and violent men among her own people will rebel in fulfillment of the vision (Daniel 11:14). Finally, a contemptible person who had not been given the honor of royalty will invade the kingdom and seize it through intrigue (Daniel 11:21). Biblical commentators identified this person as Seleucus's younger brother, Antiochus Epiphanes IV (175-164 B.C.)[17] His armed forces will rise up to desecrate the temple fortress and will abolish the daily sacrifices. Then, they will set up the abomination that causes desolation (Daniel 11:31).

From verses 36 on to the end of the chapter, the prophetic vision leaped to the end time. The earlier appearance of Antiochus Epiphanes IV seemed to foreshadow the advent of an even more ominous king who will exalt himself. Like Antiochus, he will wield enormous power, deify himself, and invade many countries including the Beautiful Land (Israel). Biblical commentators regarded this king, as the "little horn" in Daniel 7:8 and identified him as the antichrist.

At the end time, the kings of the South and the North will engage the antichrist in battle. There will be reports of armies from the east and north that will alarm him (Daniel 11:44). The conflict will finally be fought "between the seas at the beautiful holy mountain" (Daniel 11:45), probably in connection with the battle of Armageddon before the antichrist meets his end.

Here you are given a picture of the extreme debasement toward the Jewish people caused by the arrogance of Antiochus IV. The angel cautioned that even some of the wise among the Jews, God's chosen people, would stumble and turn against their God. This was a theme that echoed the prophets' warning before the demise of the Jewish's kingdom and exile to Babylon. It is a grim reminder that true religion must originate from one's authentic spiritual core. The mere presence of external traditions mandated by Mosaic laws, alone, did not insulate the Jews from turning away from their faith and God. Authentic spiritual and courageous persons like Daniel and his friends lifted the morale of his people and changed the heart of kings. In contrast, despots like Antiochus Epiphanes IV and the antichrist, despite all their might and power, will meet their fate like shadows disappearing into the middle of the night. "Yet he will come to his end, and no one will help him" (Daniel 11:45).

In this episode we are confronted by two existential questions: 1) Why does God allow suffering to occur among his people? 2) What will happen to evils in the world?

Regarding the first question, we know suffering, either personal or on a grand societal scale, is never easy to understand. If there is an almighty, omniscient and merciful God, why does He allow such events to happen? In the midst of one's personal sorrow, grief and pain, you asked, "Why does this happen to me, and to the innocent people of the world?" To persons of faith, you have this comforting words from what the angel said to Daniel, "Some of the wise will stumble, so that they may be refined, purified and made spotless until the time of the end, for it will still come at the appointed time" (Daniel 11:35). God has a purpose to allow suffering to occur--to refine, purify and make holy his people in preparation for the end time and at the appointed hours. And in conjunction with this theme, you are reminded of the Apostle Peter's exhortation:

> In this you greatly rejoice, though now for a little while you may have had to suffer grief in all kinds of trials. These have come so that your faith--of greater worth than gold, which perishes even though refined by fire--may be proved genuine and may result in praise, glory and honor when Jesus Christ is revealed. (1 Peter 1:6-7)

From a spiritual perspective, it seemed that trials and sufferings are God's ways to refine our faith so that we may rise to a higher level of spirituality. (See chapter 18)

What will happen to evils in the world? The fate of despicable despots like Antiochus IV warned evildoers to repent and humble themselves before the Lord. Despots like King Nebuchadnezzar, Belshazzar, and Antiochus IV, the antichrist, like tall trees, will be cut down. They will pass away like the morning dews. God is just and He is in control of human destiny.

Table 9. Daniel's vision of a "man in linen" and the kings of the South and the North

The Vision (Scriptural Verses)	Interpretation	Fulfillment of the Vision
Three more kings will appear in Persia (11:2).	Appearance of the three kings	1) Cambyses (530-522 B.C). 2) PseudoSmerdis or Gaumata (522) 3) Darius I (522-486)
and then a fourth, who will be far richer than all the others. When he had gained power by his wealth, he will stir up everyone against the kingdom of Greece.	Xerxes I	Xerxes 1 (486-465) who attempted to conquer Greece in 480
(3) Then a mighty king will appear, who will rule with great power and do as he pleases.	Alexander the Great	Alexander the Great (336-323)
(4) After he has appeared, his empire will be broken up and parceled out toward the four winds of heaven. It will not go to his descendants, nor will it have the power he exercised, because his empire will be uprooted and given to other.	Four divisions into which Alexander's empire fell after his untimely death in 323 B.C.	1) Macedon and Greece under Antipater and Cassander 2) Thrace and Asian Minor under Lysimachus 3) Syria under Seleucus I 4) The Holy Land and Egypt under Ptolemy I
(5) The king of the South will become strong	Ptolemy 1 Soter	Ptolemy I Soter (323-285 B.C.) of Egypt

But one of his commanders will become even stronger than he and will rule his kingdom with great power.	Seleucus 1 Nicator	Seleucus 1 Nicator (311-280 B.C.) of Syria
(6) After some years, they will become allies. The daughter of the king of the South will go to the king of the North to make an alliance, but she will not retain her power, and he and his power will not last.	King of the South: Ptolemy II Philadelphus of Egypt; his daughter, Berenice King of the North: Antiochus II Theos of Syria	A treaty was made cemented by the marriage of Berenice, daughter of Ptolemy II Philadelphus (285-246 B.C.) of Egypt to Antiochus II Theos (261-246) of Syria.
In those days, she will be handed over, together with her royal escort and her father and the one who supported her.	Berenice, her husband Antiochus, and Ptolemy, her father Laodice	Antiochus's former wife, Laodice, conspired to have Berenice and Antiochus put to death. Her father Ptolemy died at about the same time.
(7) One from her family line will arise to take her place. He will attack the forces of the king of the North and enter his fortress; he will fight against them and be victorious. (8) He will also seize their gods, their metal images and their valuable articles of silver and gold and carry them off to Egypt. For some years,	Ptolemy III Euergetes, Berenice's brother King of the North was Seleucus II Callinicus of Syria His fortress was either Seleucia which was a port of Antioch or Antioch itself	Ptolemy III Euergetes (246-221 B.C.), Berenice's brother, of Egypt, did away with Laodice. King of the North was Seleucus II Callinicus (246-226) of Syria.

he will leave the king of the North alone.		
(9-10) Then the king of the North will invade the realm of the king of the South but will retreat to his own country. His sons will prepare for war and assemble a great army, which will sweep on like an irresistible flood and carry the battle as far as his fortress.	Sons of Seleucus II: Seleucus III Ceraunus and Antiochus III (the Great) Fortress: at Raphia	Seleucus III Ceraunus (226-223) and Antiochus III (the Great) (223-187), sons of Seleucus II. His fortress was Ptolemy's fortress at Raphia (Southwest of Gaza.)
(11-12) Then the king of the South will march out in a rage and fight the king of the North, who will raise a large army, but it will be defeated. When the army is carry off, the king of the South will be filled with pride and will slaughter many thousands, yet he will not remain triumphant	King of the South: Ptolemy IV Philopator of Egypt. King of the North: Antiochus III of Syria.	Ptolemy IV Philopator (221-203 B.C.) of Egypt matched against Antiochus III and defeated him at Raphia at 217 B.C. Antiochus lost about 10,000 infantrymen at Raphia (according to Greek historian Polybus).
(13) For the king of the North will muster another army, larger than the first; and after several years, he will advance with a huge army fully equipped.	Antiochus III Epiphanes	Antiochus III Epiphanes (223-187).

(14) In those times many will rise against the king of the South, the violent men among your own people will rebel in fulfillment of the vision, but without success.	King of the South: Ptolemy V Epiphanes Violent men: Jews who joined forces of Antiochus	The Ptolemaic general Scopas crushed the rebellion in 200 B.C.
(15) Then the king of the North will come and build up siege ramps and will capture a fortified city. The forces of the South will be powerless to resist; even their best troops will not have the strength to stand.	Antiochus III Epiphanes. Fortified city: the Mediterranean port of Sidon.	Antiochus III Epiphanes captured the fortified city of Sidon.
(16) The invader will do as he pleases; no one will be able to stand against him. He will establish himself in the Beautiful Land and will have the power to destroy it.	The invader: Antiochus III Beautiful Land: the Holy Land	Antiochus III controlled the Holy Land by 197 B.C.
(17) He will determine to come with the might of his entire kingdom and will make an alliance with the king of the South. And he will give him a daughter in marriage in order to overthrow the kingdom, but his plans will not succeed or help him.	Antiochus's daughter, Cleopatra I. King of the South, Ptolemy V	Antiochus gave his daughter Cleopatra I in marriage to Ptolemy V in 194 B.C.

(18) Then he will turn his attention to the coastlands and will take many of them, but a commander will put an end to his insolence and will turn his insolence back on him.	He: Antiochus Coastland: Asia Minor and perhaps also mainland Greece. Commander: The Roman consul Lucius Cornelius Scipio Asiaticus	The Roman consul Lucius Cornelius Scipio Asiaticus defeated Antiochus at Magnesia in Asian Minor in 190 B.C.
(19) After this, he will turn back toward the fortresses of his own country but will stumble and fall, to be seen no more.	Antiochus III	Antiochus III died in 187 B.C. while attempting to plunder a temple in the province of Elymais.
(20) His successor will send out a tax collector to maintain the royal splendor. In a few years, however, he will be destroyed, yet not in anger or in battle.	His successor: Seleucus IV Philopator. Tax collector: Heliodorus, Seleucus's finance minister	Antiochus's successor, Seleucus IV Philopator (187-175 B.C.). Heliodorus, Seleucus's finance minister, engineered a conspiracy against Seleucus who became its victim.
(21) He will be succeeded by a contemptible person who has not been given the honor of royalty. He will invade the kingdom when its people feel secure, and he will seize it through intrigue.	Contemptible person: Seleucus's younger brother Antiochus IV Epiphanes.	Seleucus's younger brother Antiochus IV Epiphanes (175-164 B.C.) seized power while the rightful heir to the throne, Demetrius I, son of Seleucus, was still very young. Antiochus invaded Syro-Palestine.

(22) Then an overwhelming army will be swept away before him; both it and a prince of the covenant will be destroyed.	Prince of the covenant was either the high priest Onias III or Ptolemy VI Philometor (181-146) of Egypt.	The high priest Onias III was murdered in 170 B.C. Ptolemy VI Philometor (181-146) of Egypt, translated Hebrew phrase means "confederate king."
(23) After coming to an agreement with him, he will act deceitfully, and with only a few people he will rise to power.	He: Antiochus IV	Antiochus IV Epiphanes
(24) When the richest provinces feel secure, he will invade them and will achieve what neither his fathers nor his forefathers did. He will distribute plunder, loot and wealth among his followers. He will plot the overthrow of fortresses—but only for a time.	Riches province referred either to the Holy Land or to Egypt Fortresses, Egypt.	Antiochus invaded Egypt.
(25-26) With a large army he will stir up his strength and courage against the king of the South. The king of the South will wage war with a large and very powerful army, but he will not be able to stand because of the plots devised against him.	King of the South: Ptolemy VI.	Ptolemy VI waged war against Antiochus but was not successful.

Those who eat from the king's provisions will try to destroy him; his army will be swept away, and many will fall in battle.		
(27-28) The two kings, with their hearts bent on evil, will sit at the same table and lie to each other, but to no avail, because an end will still come at the appointed time. The king of the North will return to his own country with great wealth, but his heart will be set against the holy covenant. He will take action against it and then return to his own country.	Two kings, Antiochus IV and Ptolemy VI	Two kings, Antiochus and Ptolemy who was living in Antiochus's custody. Antiochus IV in 169 B.C., plundered the temple in Jerusalem, set up a garrison there and massacred many Jews in the city.
(29-30) At the appointed time he will invade the South again, but this time the outcome will be different from what it was before. [30] Ships of the western coastlands will oppose him, and he will lose heart. Then he will turn back and vent his fury against the holy covenant. He will return and show favor to those who forsake the holy covenant.	Ships of the western coastline: Roman vessels under the command of Popilius Laenus. Those who forsake the holy covenant: Apostate Jews	From the western coastlands. Roman vessels under the command of Popilius Laenus opposed Antiochus.

(31-32) His armed forces will rise up to desecrate the temple fortress and will abolish the daily sacrifice. Then they will set up the abomination that causes desolation. With flattery he will corrupt those who have violated the covenant, but the people who know their God will firmly resist him.	Antiochus IV People who know God: Maccabees	Abomination that causes desolation: Antiochus set up the altar to the Pagan god Zeus Olympus in 168 B.C. This prefigured a similar abomination that Jesus predicted will be erected (See Matt 24:15; Lk 21:20). The persecution of Jews under Antiochus led to the emergence of the Maccabees (Hasmonaens).] (New Unger Bible, 793)
(33-35) Those who are wise will instruct many, though for a time they will fall by the sword or be burned or captured or plundered. When they fall, they will receive a little help, and many who are not sincere will join them. Some of the wise will stumble, so that they may be refined, purified and made spotless until the time of the end, for it will still come at the appointed time.	Those who are wise: The Hasidim. A little help: the guerilla uprising under the leadership of Mattathias and his son Judas Maccabeus. Time of the end: the more distant future.	The godly leaders of the Jewish resistance movement, also called the Hasidim. A little help: The early success of the guerilla uprising (168 B.C.) that originated in Modein, 17 miles northwest of Jerusalem, under the leadership of Mattathias and his son Judas Maccabeus. In December, 165 B.C., the altar of the temple was rededicated. Time of the end: Daniel concludes his prediction about Antiochus and begins to prophecy concerning the more distant future.

(36) The king will do as he pleases. He will exalt and magnify himself above every god and will say unheard-of things against the God of gods. He will be successful until the time of wrath is completed, for what has been determined must take place.	The antichrist	From here to the end of ch.11, the antichrist is in view. The details of the description do not fit Antiochus IV Epiphanes.
(37) He will show no regard for the gods of his ancestors or for the one desired by women, nor will he regard any god, but will exalt himself above them all.	Tammuz or the Messiah	The one desired by women: Tammuz or the Messiah
(38-39) Instead of them, he will honor a god of fortresses; a god unknown to his fathers he will honor with gold and silver, with precious stones and costly gifts. He will attack the mightiest fortresses with the help of a foreign god and will greatly honor those who acknowledge him. He will make them rulers over many people and will distribute the land at a price.	The antichrist	The antichrist
(40-45) At the time of the end the king of the South will engage him	The antichrist and his political enemies.	Conflicts to be waged between the antichrist and his political enemies.

in battle, and the king of the North will storm out against him with chariots and cavalry and a great fleet of ships. He will invade many countries and sweep through them like a flood. He will also invade the Beautiful Land. Many countries will fall, but Edom, Moab and the leaders of Ammon will be delivered from his hand. He will extend his power over many countries; Egypt will not escape. He will gain control of the treasures of gold and silver and all the riches of Egypt, with the Libyans and Nubians in submission. But reports from the east and the north will alarm him, and he will set out in a great rage to destroy and annihilate many. He will pitch his royal tents between the seas at the beautiful holy mountain. Yet he will come to his end, and no one will help him.	"at the beautiful holy mountain", Jerusalem's temple mount	He will meet his end "at the beautiful holy mountain", Jerusalem's temple mount, perhaps in connection with the battle of Armageddon.

Source. *Adapted from* Zondervan NIV Study Bible (Fully Revised), Copyright© 1985, 1995, 2002 by Zondervan), 1336-1340.

Chapter 11. KEY POINTS

1. Daniel had a vision of a series of wars between the Ptolemy's [king of the South] and the Seleucids [king of the North] following Alexander's death that greatly affected Israelites and Jerusalem.

2. A contemptible person, identified as Seleucus's younger brother, Antiochus Epiphanes IV will seize power and invade Israel. He will desecrate the temple fortress, abolish the Jewish daily sacrifices, and set up the "abomination that causes desolation."

3. The vision also predicted that during the end time, an even more ominous king than Antiochus Epiphanes IV would appear. This latter king, identified as the antichrist, will exalt himself, wield enormous power, deify himself, and invade many countries including the Beautiful Land [Israel].

4. At the end time, it was predicted that the battle of Armageddon would be fought between the antichrist, the kings of the South and the North, and armies from the east and north, before the antichrist meets his end.

5. Daniel's psychospirituality was reflected in his willingness to allow God to convey vision through him that predicted futuristic world events.

CHAPTER 12

The End Times

Those who are wise will shine like the brightness of
heavens, and those who lead many to righteousness,
like the stars for ever [sic] and ever (Daniel 12:3)

C hapter 12 is a postlude. It started with an announcement
that the archangel, Michael, the great prince who protects
the people of Israel, will arise during the end time. There
will be great distress. And it ended with comforting messages conveyed to Daniel and his people.

But at that time your people--those everyone whose name
is found written in the book will be delivered. Multitudes
who sleep in the dust of the earth will awake: some to
everlasting life, others to shame and everlasting contempt.
Those who are wise will shine like the brightness of the
heavens, and those who lead many to righteousness like the
stars for ever and ever. (Daniel 12:2-4) (See table 10)

You will note here that the resurrection of the dead was specifically mentioned. Daniel was told to close up and seal the words of the
scroll until the end of time. As he looked up, he saw two other angels,
one standing on each side of the Tigris River, asking the "man dressed

in linen", "How long will it be before these astonishing things are fulfilled?" The "man dressed in linen" answered that it will be for "a time, times and half a time. When the power of the holy people has been finally broken, all these things will be complete"(Daniel 12:7).

Daniel heard and again, did not understand. It was a mystery that was kept even from him. The prophecy will be closed until the end of time. And Daniel was told, "from the time that the daily sacrifice is abolished and the abomination that causes desolation is set up, there will be 1,290 days. Blessed is the one who waits for and reaches till the end of 1,335 days" (Daniel 12:11).

Regarding the interpretation of the 1,290 and 1,335 days, John Phillips in his book, *Exploring The Future*, opined that these two periods (1,290 and 1,335 days) seemed to have a correspondence with what actually happened when Antiochus Epiphanes IV (the archetype of antichrist) desecrated Jerusalem (Phillips, p. 56). From the time of the desecration of Jerusalem to its restoration by Judas Maccabaeus, there were 1,290 days. From the restoration of Jerusalem to Antiochus' death and the end of his persecution was another 45 days, making a total of 1,335 days [1,290 + 45 =1,335].[18] Phillips reasoned that when the antichrist sets up the "abomination that causes desolation" by desecrating the temple in Jerusalem, "that will signal for the commencement of the Great Tribulation, which will end 1,260 days later at the return of Christ at Armageddon."[19] Meanwhile, "45 days might be allowed for the mopping-up operations and the convening of the great assize in the valley of Jehoshaphat and perhaps allowing time for the ceremonial cleansing of the land of Israel to prepare for the Jewish remnant for their coming role as leaders of the world affairs during the millennium before Christ begins his glorious millennial reign."[20] Hence, "Blessed is the one who waits for and reaches the end of the 1,335 days" (Daniel 12:11-12).

As for Daniel, the man esteemed by God who had received these words, he was told to go his way till the end. He will rest, and then at the end of time, will rise to receive his allotted inheritance

(Daniel 12:13). Daniel, in the end, is a mortal like all of us. The final reward for his spirituality is the resurrection in the last day to receive God's eternal inheritance. Just as St. Paul had affirmed for all Christians, "And you also were included in Christ when you heard the word of truth, the gospel of your salvation. Having believed, you were marked in him with a seal, the promise of the Holy Spirit, who is a deposit guaranteeing our inheritance until the redemption of those who are God's possession–to the praise of his glory" (Ephesians 1:13).

With Daniel's prophetic tasks completed, the angel Michael left us a challenging message: "the wise will shine like the brightness of heavens, and those who lead many to righteousness like the stars for ever and ever…Many will go here and there to increase knowledge" (Daniel 12:3). Who are the wise? Who will set his/her mind to gain understanding and to humble himself/herself before God as Daniel did? Who will lead others to righteousness?

Table 10. Daniel's vision of the end time

Vision (Scriptural Verses)	Interpretation
(12:1) At that time Michael, the great prince who protects your people, will arise. There will be a time of distress such as has not happened from the beginning of nations until then. But at that time your people—everyone whose name is found written in the book—will be delivered.	A warning to God's people of the coming distress and the promise of eventual deliverance
(2) Multitudes who sleep in the dust of the earth will awake; some to everlasting life, others to shame and everlasting contempt.	First clear reference to resurrection of both the righteous and the wicked. The phrase *everlasting life* occurs only here in the OT.

(3-4) Those who are wise will shine like the brightness of the heavens, and those who lead many to righteousness, like the stars for ever and ever. But you, Daniel, close up and seal the words of the scroll until the time of the end. Many will go here and there to increase knowledge."	An exhortation to the wise to lead the unrighteous to God. Daniel was told to conclude his prophecy.
(5) Then I, Daniel, looked, and there before me stood two others, one on this bank of the river and one on the opposite bank.	Two was the minimum number of witnesses to an oath.
(6-7) One of them said to the man clothed in linen, who was above the waters of the river, "How long will it be before these astonishing things are fulfilled?" The man clothed in linen, who was above the waters of the river, lifted his right hand and his left hand toward heaven, and I heard him swear by him who lives forever, saying, "It will be for a time, times and half a time. When the power of the holy people has been finally broken, all these things will be completed."	The time it will take for the fulfillment of the prophecy: Time, time and a half
(8-10) I heard, but I did not understand. So I asked, "My lord, what will the outcome of all this be?" He replied, "Go your way, Daniel, because the words are closed up and sealed until the time of the end. Many will be purified, made spotless and refined, but the wicked will continue to be wicked. None of the wicked will understand, but those who are wise will understand.	Daniel was puzzled by the prophecy and wanted to know its outcome. He was told that the prophecy is sealed.

(11-12) "From the time that the daily sacrifice is abolished and the abomination that causes desolation is set up, there will be 1,290 days. Blessed is the one who waits for and reaches the end of the 1,335 days. (13) "As for you, go your way till the end. You will rest, and then at the end of the days you will rise to receive your allotted inheritance."	"Apparently representing either (1) further calculations relating to the persecutions of Antiochus Epiphanes or (2) further end-time calculations.

Source. *Adapted from* Zondervan NIV Study Bible (Fully Revised), Copyright© 1985, 1995, 2002 by Zondervan), 1339-1340.

Chapter 12. KEY POINTS

1. The archangel Michael, the great prince who protects the people of Israel, will arise during the end time. There will be great distress. But those whose name is found written in the book will be delivered.

2. The resurrection of the dead was mentioned--some to everlasting life, others to shame and everlasting contempt.

3. Daniel was told to close up and seal the words of the scroll until the end of time that was predicted to be "a time, times and half a time."

4. Daniel was told the outcome of all of these "from the time that the daily sacrifice is abolished and the abomination that causes desolation is set up, there will be 1,290 days. Blessed is the one who waits for and reaches till the end of 1,335 days"

5. Those who are wise will shine like the brightness of the heavens, and those who lead many to righteousness like the stars forever and ever.

6. Being reassured by God to go his way till the end, will rise again and receive his allotted inheritance, confirmed Daniel's psychospirituality.

INTERIM SUMMARY

Part 1

ENCOUNTER WITH THE BABYLONIAN
AND PERSIAN KINGS:
THE OBJECTIVE MANIFESTATION OF
DANIEL'S PSYCHOSPIRITUALITY

The first 6 chapters of Daniel depicted Daniel's encounter with the Babylonian and Persian kings and their wise men. What were the objective evidences of Daniel's psychospirituality and what did they reveal?

Early in his youth, Daniel had already resolved that he would remain steadfast in his faith, to say no to things that might impinge on the purity of his soul and the integrity of his character. He was not going to compromise his morality and values. His resoluteness in faith pleased God and God gave him (and his friends) knowledge and understanding of all kinds of literature and learning. And Daniel could understand visions and dreams of all kinds (Daniel 1:17). Daniel's faith and spirituality pervaded all his subsequent behavior. His moral fortitude earned him the respect of his gentile supervisor. It most likely emboldened his friends to stand fast on their beliefs in the face of death. He surrounded himself with trustworthy friends of steadfast faith who also were his loyal prayer partners. Through all political intrigues and dangers that lurked in the king's court, Daniel was wise and knew how to conduct himself diplomatically and tactfully. His impeccable character, intelligence, efficiency, effectiveness, and fierce loyalty to his kings earned him their trust, so that he was placed in a position of power to act for his people when the occasion arose (See chapter 9).

Daniel's psychospirituality was firmly rooted in a faith that was revealed in all aspects of his life. What made him esteemed by both God and men? It had to do with his psychospirituality reflected in his humility and resoluteness to seek and serve God.

The conscious will to seek God with a humble spirit invited God's blessing and created a powerful reservoir of psychospiritual energy for Daniel. Daniel used his moral and spiritual energies to honor God and benefit his people. His life was a living testament on how God can use people, including intelligent public servants, who are willing to become vessels of blessings to others.

Daniel's faith was tested to become refined gold. Starting from his youth, he went through incredible amounts of trials that climaxed in his being thrown into the lions' den. He clung to God all through-out his trials, and God stood by him. When you made a conscious choice to serve God, God may refine you to become "pure gold" in order to become God's effective instrument. That may include allow-ing you to go through trials of suffering.

Part 2

DANIEL'S DREAMS AND VISIONS:

THE SUBJECTIVE MANIFESTATION OF DANIEL'S PSYCHOSPIRITUALITY

The last 6 chapters revealed a range of incredible visions and events that focused on three major parties: God, Israel, and Daniel. Since dreams and visions are presumably derived from the unconscious mind, symbolism was used and its meaning required interpretation. Images from the unconscious mind often conflict with the conscious mind. In Daniel's case, we have no hint of any sexual or aggressive impulses seeking discharge. Rather, Daniel's conflict involved mostly apocalyptical moral and spiritual issues. His wish and love for Israel, on one hand, and the devastation to Israel that he learned through vision, on the other hand, epitomized the struggles of his conscious and unconscious mind. The struggles involved both the terrestrial and heavenly realm. At the terrestrial level, you will note:

- The prophecy about the fate of early gentile empires and their impact on Israel.
- Daniel's plea to God for the restoration of Judah and Jerusalem.
- The battles for supremacy among Alexander the Great's generals following Alexander's death.
- The appearances of two "small horns" (Antiochus Epiphanes IV and the antichrist) at different time that will cause extreme devastation to Israel.
- The great battles at the end time between the antichrist and the armies of the south, north and east.
- The advent of the everlasting kingdom of God after the end of the world.

At the heavenly realm, you have noted visions regarding:
- The glory of God, the Ancient of Day.
- The appearance of the "son of man" coming with the clouds of heaven.
- The appearance of the angel Michael and Gabriel conveying messages to Daniel, and hinting on heavenly struggles with Satan.

DANIEL'S VISION OF THE WORLD'S DESTINY

Daniel's prophecies covered a period that spanned from King Nebuchadnezzar's reign (605 B.C.) to the end of time. These prophecies related the fate of the gentile worlds as well as the nation of Israel.

References to Daniel's vision of the world were found in the following scriptural passages:

Daniel's interpretation of King Nebuchadnezzar's dream of the huge stature (chapter 2).

Daniel's vision of the 4 beasts (chapter 7).

Daniel's vision of a Ram and a Goat (chapter 8).

Daniel's Vision of the "seventy 'sevens'" (chapter 9).

Fig 2. is a schematic presentation of Daniel's view of world's history.

FIGURE 2. Trajectory of the human destiny as prophesied by Daniel and related events

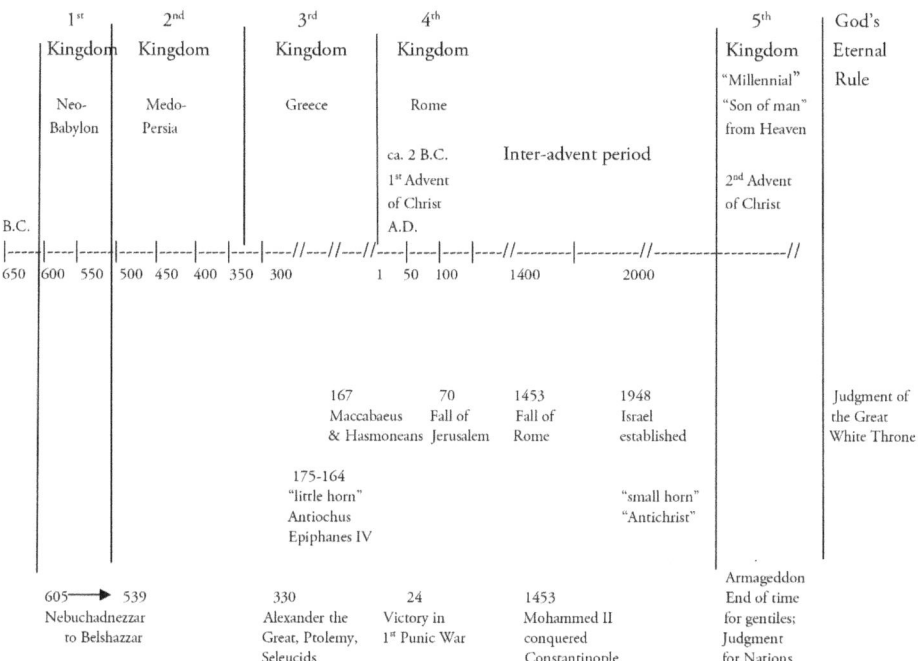

Source. *Adapted from* Zondervan NIV Study Bible (Fully Revised), Copyright© 1985.1995,2002 by Zondervan.

FULFILLMENT OF DANIEL'S PROPHESIES

The veracity of prophecy is reflected in its fulfillment. Table 11 showed the status of the fulfillment of Daniel's prophecies. Chapters 1, 3, and 6 had no prophetic significance. Many of the prophecies concerning the gentile world (chapters 2, 4, 6, 7) and that affect Israel (chapters 7, 8, 9, 10, 11) had already been fulfilled, some during Daniel's time but most of them after his death. A large section of Daniel's prophecies were related to events at the end of time (chapter 2, 7, 9, 10, 11, 12). These remained unfulfilled. Still unfolding and may have relevance to our current world events were the descriptions of the world's conflicts (chapter 11), the predictions of the appearance of the antichrist symbolized by the "little horn" in chapter 7 who will cause the "abomination that causes desolation" and as the future "king who will exalt himself" (chapter 11).

DANIEL'S PRAYER AND HIS VISION OF THE SEVENTY "7S" (CHAPTER 9)

In chapter 9, you have noted that the angel Gabriel gave the interpretation of the meaning of the seventy "7s". Jeremiah's prophecy of the end of the desolation of Jerusalem after seventy years (Jeremiah 25:12, 29:10, 32:37-38) was fulfilled when the Persian King Cyrus decreed to allow the Israelites to return to Judah to rebuild the temple of Jerusalem (Ezra 1:1-4). At that time, Daniel was serving in King Cyrus's court.

Furthermore, you will note that part of the prophecy of the seventy '7s' (483 years), the period of 434 years that spanned from the time of authorizing the rebuilding of Jerusalem (Ezra 7:1) to the coming of the Messiah and his crucifixion, and the period of 49 years from the crucifixion to the destruction of Jerusalem by the Roman Emperor Titus in 70 A.D., had been fulfilled with remarkable accuracy.[21]

A final "7" years referring to events at the end time remained unfulfilled (See chapter 9), and has been the subject of eschatological explorations.

DANIEL'S EMOTIONAL RESPONSE TO VISIONS AND ITS MEANING

The book of Daniel contained a huge section of narrative devoted to his emotional reactions to dreams, visions and events (See table 8).

You have noted that the paradox of Daniel's helpless emotional reactions in the last 6 chapters were in marked contrast to the assertive, bold, confident, erudite, and wise behavioral demeanor displayed earlier before King Nebuchadnezzar, Belshazzar, and Cyrus. Earlier, I have alluded to some of the psychological struggles between Daniel's conscious and unconscious mind that may underlie this paradox. (See also chapter 13) But there seemed to be a larger moral and spiritual picture that may have under laid this paradox.

1. The confrontation with the gentile kings was meant to reveal Jehovah's might over and above the gentile gods. The visions also had awesome revelations. The images of the fate of the gentile empires symbolized by the ferocious four beasts (chapter 7), the ram and the goat (chapter 8), the vision of the Great Wars between the kings of the North and South, and their impact on Israel, were experiences beyond human comprehension. These were intended only for Daniel to experience and know. Daniel chose to write them down for posterity.

2. Daniel was not in a position to reveal his visions to his superior and to his people. It was neither politically expedient nor appropriate. Daniel literally was troubled, became sick, and almost died from these experiences. He could only keep the visions to himself while he went about doing the king's business. He realized that God had only

wanted him to know. He knew a lot but had to tolerate undue emotional strain just to seek God's revelation and to keep the revelations to himself. Yet, Daniel was determined to continue seeking God's will despite the emotional challenge that will impose on him. His forceful will and humility before God gave us an appreciation of his deep psychospirituality.

3. The revelation of the awesome images of God's glory, the "son of man", and the angels defied human understanding. These visions provoked extreme fear in Daniel. You can surmise that when human beings, even beloved servant and holy prophets of God like Daniel, had glimpse of the heavenly glory, it was just too much to behold. God's glorious holiness would reflect upon and reveal man's sinfulness and deficiencies. And this could be devastating.

4. God's reassurance. God sent his angels to touch Daniel, lift him off the ground, and respond to his prayer and petition. These were novel experiences for Daniel. God revealed much of the world's future to Daniel and promised to reward him for his role as an instrument and conveyer of His will. The angel told him of his eventual heavenly inheritance. Throughout the whole process of God's revelation and Daniel's emotional reactions, Daniel willingly and humbly submitted himself to these severe emotional experiences. At the same time, the Almighty God did not leave His messenger helpless and unattended. God sent His angels to convey His reassuring words and extended His comforting hand.

Daniel was made to understand very clearly it was God's prerogative to do as He pleases, a theme that the books of Job and Jonah also conveyed. It was not up to mortals to question God's motive and timing. God is both just and merciful. This is reflected in God's dealing with Daniel. God through Daniel shows you that He is in control over events of the world, and your personal life. While going through trials and tribulation, you could be reminded that God still cares and will protect (See chapters 18-20). Hence, at the conclusion of chapter 12, Daniel was told to seal the prophecy. Further revelations will come later as revealed in the books of Revelation in the New Testament. His mission accomplished, God promised Daniel resurrection and eternal inheritance. What a message of hope for the people of God!

Table 11. Fulfillment of Daniel's Prophecies

Daniel's Prophecy, Symbolism And Its Representation	Status of Fulfillment	Reference
1. Nebuchadnezzar's Dream Of The Huge Stature		Chapter 2 2:32,36
• Head of Gold: Neo-Babylon	Fulfilled	2:32,39
• Chest and Arms of silver: Medo-Persia	Fulfilled Fulfilled	2:32,39 2:33,40
• Belly and thighs of bronze: Greece	Fulfilled	
• Legs of iron: Roman Empire Antichrist	Unfulfilled	2:34,44
• Rock that destroys the statues: Kingdom of God	Unfulfilled	
2. Nebuchadnezzar's Dream Of A Big Tree	Fulfilled	Chapter 4
3. Belshazzar's Vision Of The Handwriting On The Wall	Fulfilled	Chapter 5
4. Vision of the Four beasts		Chapter 7
• Lion : Neo-Babylon	Fulfilled	7:4
• Bear: Medo-Persia	Fulfilled	7:5
• Leopard: Greece	Fulfilled	7:6
• Terrifying and Frightening Beast: Rome	Fulfilled Unfulfilled	7:7 7:8,23
• Another horn, a lit- tle one: Antichrist	Unfulfilled	7:9, 27
• Ancient of Days: Eternal Kingdom of the Saints		

5. Vision of Ram and Goat		Chapter 8
• Ram: Medo-Persia	Fulfilled	8:20
• Goat: King of Greece	Fulfilled	8:21
6. Daniel's Prayer and His Visions of the 70 "Sevens"		Chapter 9 9:2,
• Jeremiah's Prophecy of the returning Jewish exiles to rebuild Jerusalem	Fulfilled	Jeremiah 25:11-12
• 70 "Sevens" (490 years): First 69 "sevens" (7 + 62 =69 or 483 years) Period from the time of authorizing the rebuilding of Jerusalem and the coming of the Messiah.	Fulfilled	9:24 9:25
1. 7 "Sevens" (49 years): Period of the complete restoration of Jerusalem.		
2. 62 "Sevens" (434 years): Period from the restoration of Jerusalem to the coming of the Messiah.		
3. Cutting Off the Anointed One: Crucifixion of Christ	Fulfilled	9:26
4. An indeterminate period between the 69th and the 70th "seven", a period of war and desolation.	Unfolding	
Final "seven": appearance of the "little horn" orantichrist who sets up "the abomination thatcauses desolation."	Unfulfilled	9:26-27
7. Vision of a Man Dressed in Linen: • Resurrected Christ		Chapter 10; Revelations 1:12-16

• Three Persian Kings: Darius, the Medes (530-522 B.C.; Pseudo-Smerdis or Gaumata (522); Darius 1 (522-486) who attempted to conquer Greece in 480.	Fulfilled	Chapter 11:2
• A mighty king: Alexander the Great	Fulfilled	11:3
• His empire broken up and parceled out towards the four winds: Empires divided up among Alexander's four generals.	Fulfilled	11:4; 7:4-7
• King of the South: Ptolemy I Soter (323-285 B.C.) of Egypt	Fulfilled	11:11
• King of the North: Antiochus III (223-187 B.C.)	Fulfilled	11:11
• Contemptible Person: Antiochus Epiphanes IV	Fulfilled	11:21
• The King Who Exalts Himself: The antichrist	Evolving	11:36-45
8. The End Time		Chapter 12
• A time of great distress	Unfulfilled	12:1
• Multitudes who sleep in the dust of the earth will awake: Resurrection of both the righteous and the wicked to face God's judgment	Unfulfilled	12:2
• Period of the astonishing things are fulfilled: Period from the time that the daily sacrifice is abolished and the abomination that causes desolation is set up --1,290 days	Unfulfilled	12:11; Matthews 24:15 Luke 21:20

• You will rest and then at the end of the days you will rise to receive your allotted inheritance: Personal reference to Daniel's resurrection at end time	Unfulfilled	12:13

Source. *Adapted from* Zondervan NIV Study Bible (Fully Revised), Copyright© 1985.1995,2002 by Zondervan.

PART 3

10 Lessons to Empower

Your Life

CHAPTER 13

The Power To Say No: Aligning Your Conscious And Unconscious Mind

The eye is the lamp of the body. If your eyes are good,
your whole body will be full of light (Matthew 6:22)

INTRODUCTION

In Part One, you have noted how Daniel encountered the challenges of the Babylonian and Persian kings and their cohorts. The challenges to his faith, struggles for personal survival and adjustment in a foreign land, and his behavioral response, can be said to have involved primarily decisions of his conscious mind. In Part Two, Daniel faced challenges of a different kind: how would he respond to God's conveyance of His will through his dreams and visions regarding the fate of the nation of Israel and the gentile world? Daniel had to struggle with images that emerged from his deep unconscious mind. These incredible dreams and visions sapped his psychic energies and emotions. Yet, he persisted in seeking God's will, despite at high personal emotional costs. The results of these struggles of both his conscious and unconscious mind were remarkable: his faith was strengthened, his people were able to return to Judah and rebuild Jerusalem, God's will was conveyed and His name elevated. The alignment of both his conscious and unconscious mind empowered him. You, too, can be empowered to change.

If you've ever felt helpless to change things--to quit smoking, reduce weight, overcome alcoholism, foster a more loving relation- ship, lower your blood pressure, change a dead-end job, or lift your- self out of depression or deep anxiety--you're not alone. Helplessness is ubiquitous. Even St. Paul did not escape it. Consider his experi- ence, "I do not understand what I do. For what I want to do I do not do, but what I hate I do" (Romans 7:15).

From a spiritual perspective, Paul was not talking about super- ficial conflicts. He was addressing deep psychospiritual issues within your being--your soul, your nature, food, sex, power, money, desires, personality flaws, etc.--issues that could weigh you down and pull you in opposite direction against your ego ideal. Paul said there is a "law" of the flesh, reinforced by the Mosaic law, embodied in the concept of the "old Adam", whose nature is sinful and the result is death (Romans 7:14-20; 1Corinthians 15:22). The law of the flesh constantly works against the law of the spirit. Thus, the conflict could cause you to feel torn, indecisive, ambivalent, restless, and neurotic. These desires of the flesh could become your demons. To overcome these demons, Paul asserted that you have to be liberated from your "old self", crucify the "old Adam", and become a new person, through faith in Christ. (Romans 3:21-24; Galatians 2:20) This spiritual process of transformation is akin to a spiritual new birth, as Jesus told Nicodemus (John 3:3, 5-8). The implication is that though faith in Christ, a new nature of the "self" will evolve, whose characteristics may involve changes in your whole personal- ity–thinking, feeling, and behavior (2 Corinthians 5:17) manifesting as "fruits of the Spirit" (Galatians 5:22) and a new God-centered mindset (2 Peter 1:5-7).

From a psychological perspective, the process of change may encompass the total remaking of both your conscious and unconscious mind. Otherwise, Christian messages become just an intellectual exercise. To be empowered, the transformative power of the Christian message must reach your innermost being, to create the wellspring of living water from your soul.

This is what psycho-spiritual empowerment entails, the coming together of both your conscious and unconscious mind, to be free as much as possible of neurotic conflicts so that you can decide, as Daniel did, to be free and be on the side of the angel. Here are 4 steps on how to align your conscious and unconscious mind:

STEP 1. RECOGNIZING THE REALITY OF THE UNCONSCIOUS.

The unconscious is that part of your mind that is beyond conscious recognition during waking hours. Yet, it plays an important part in your motivation. The unconscious manifests itself in dream and vision. But during waking hours, it intrudes through absent-minded tasks, slips of the tongue, the so-called "lies" of the hysterics, and the denials of the neurotics. What some people don't realize or accept is the reality of the unconscious. But in fact, both the conscious and unconscious minds are linked. As psychoanalyst Carl Jung had explicated, "A multitude of temporarily obscured thoughts, impressions, and images, that, in spite of being lost, continue to influence our conscious mind."[22] Faith-based individuals, including Christian, are no exception. If there is a disconnection between conscious and unconscious motives, it may create conflict and cause behavioral paradoxes. This may explain why some tele-evangelists, though eloquent, stumbled in their private lives. Empires built by ambitious pastors only to be sadly crumbled and fell by greed, pride, sex, the lust for power, or mismanagement. Without real change from within, you can be fooled by your intellect rationalizing Christian precept. You may think you've changed, but in reality, your basic character remains the same. Christ pointed out this paradox when he said,

"Not everyone who says to me, 'Lord, Lord,' will enter the kingdom of heaven, but only those who does the will of my Father who is in heaven" (Matthew 7:25).

Carl Jung felt that human is powerless because of possession by powers beyond his control. Jung, of course is referring to the power of the unconscious psyche (mind), that archetypes, "dynamic nuclei of the psyche", whose workings often contradict the conscious mind.

> "…[Contemporary man] is blind to the fact that, with all his rationality and efficiency, he is possessed by 'powers' that are beyond his control. His gods and demons have not disappeared at all; they have merely got new names. They keep him on the run with restlessness, vague comprehensions, psychological complications, an insatiable need for pills, alcohol, tobacco, food—and above all, an impressive array of neurosis."[23]

To be truly empowered, you have to rid the demons in your unconscious. We do not have data what young Daniel's unconscious mind was like at the time when he resolved to refuse the king's food and wine. But judging from his actions throughout his life, and his emotional struggle when he received God's visions (See part 2), his mind can be said to have exhibited a "triumph of the soul." Daniel was persistent in consciously seeking God's revelation. Confronted by dream and vision, he had to struggle unconsciously, too. But Daniel emerged each time from his experience stronger than before. And God rewarded him with wisdom and knowledge that guided him the rest of his life (Daniel 1:17).

True change involves the alignment of your conscious and unconscious mind, the psychological and spiritual. Daniel set the example to say no to harm, and yes to God through psychospiritual commitment.

STEP 2. RIDDING THE DEMONS. LOOKING WITHIN YOURSELF AND REMOVING THE "PLANK IN YOUR EYE."

In his Sermon on the Mount, Jesus preached to his disciples and crowd saying, "The eye is the lamp of the body. If your eyes are good, your whole body will be full of light" (Matthew 6:22). Further on, he added, "Why do you look at the speck of sawdust in your brother's eye and pay no attention to the plank in your own eye?" (Matthew 7:3). "You hypocrite, first take the plank out of your eye, and then you will see clearly to remove the speck from your brother's eye" (Matthew 7:5).

Jesus was using metaphors to clearly convey the essential of *knowing yourself* for self-growth in order to be *effective* in helping others.

Mental health professionals, pastors, ministers, teachers, and counselors are engaged in tasks to help people changed. For some individuals, hearing a lecture or a sermon, taking in an advice from a psychotherapist may be enough to induce change. Yet, change comes slowly for most people, if at all, particularly in areas involving personality flaws. To achieve a level of change that is more permanent, it requires time, effort, and repeated practice. Many times, outside professional help is needed. Psychotherapy, psychoanalysis, and cognitive behavioral therapy are procedures aimed to assist in uncovering our demons hidden in the unconscious. The assumption is that when unconscious material are made conscious, the ego is then in a better position to decide what to do with the uncovered material. And that is the beginning of empowerment and wisdom. Let me share with you a personal experience at midlife.

Safe in a psychiatric career, and working as a staff psychiatrist in a veteran hospital in Massachusetts, having a wonderful wife and a child, and living comfortably at Lexington, Massachusetts, I had most of what I had dreamed for before coming over to this wonderful country from the Philippines. Yet, I wasn't happy. A deep restlessness kept bothering me. Knowing the working of the unconscious, I turned to psychoanalysis to uncover the roots of my unhappiness. On the couch, I uncovered my unresolved grief about my mother who passed away in her fifties, two years after I left Manila. Psychoanalysis helped me to resolve a major part of my grief. It also gave me insight into issue of my self-esteem. It confronted me with my prejudices and distortion of my perception of other people. It enlightened me on why I couldn't concentrate and sustain projects that I had started. These unresolved issues were my demons. After three and half years on the couch, I was happier, able to better focus on my professional interest, and eventually produced my first book on cross-cultural psychiatry. I felt empowered to confront my neuroticism and ambivalence, to say no to things that distracted my goals and drained my energies, and yes to things that made me happy and gave meanings to my life. It didn't debunk my belief in God (sorry, Freud). Instead, analytic experience fostered in me a clearer, keener sense of the unconscious that complemented my broader view of religious and existential issues. After coming to California, it led me to return to my first love, my religious roots, my Christian faith, and the practical meaning of biblical applications to real life situations. I felt a passion to connect the wonderful lessons gleaned from the disciplines of neurobiology, psychology, anthropology, and spirituality. This passion led me to the study of biblical characters. Thus, after publishing three books on cross-cultural psychiatry, I published my first book on psychospirituality, the *Eyes of the Heart: The Biblical Path to Spirituality and Empowerment.* The current volume, *Empowered*, is the second.

In the early 60's, psychiatric residents were strongly encouraged to seek psychotherapy or psychoanalysis for two reasons: 1) to remove the personal "planks", i.e., countertransference issues that stem from the therapist's own background which may intrude and/ or impede on the doctor-patient relationship, and 2) to acquire fine-tuned psychotherapeutic technique. Jesus's admonition on how the eye will illuminate the whole body has this connotation--to remove first your "planks." Once you gained insights attained through the "eyes of your heart", then your whole life will have a clearer vision (See reference 118). Have the courage to look within yourself, as Daniel did, to rid the demons in your unconscious, to break free from the indecisiveness, ambivalence, and fears that may be hindering your decisions, and hampering your self-growth and happiness.

STEP 3. TRANSFORMING THE MEANING OF YOUR LIFE'S EXPERIENCE. ALIGNING YOUR EGO IDEALS WITH THAT OF CHRIST'S.

Research has shown how you appraise any situation affects how you feel.[24] The optimist sees the "cup always is half full", while the pessimist sees it, "half empty." This makes a whole difference in how you cope with stress, whether you are vulnerable to depression or anxiety attacks, or not. In fact, these attitudes may potentially affect your gene life as well (See chapter 21). Consider the following metaphors and how they can transform your life.

- Your life is now linked with Christ. Paul said, "I have been crucified with Christ and I no longer live, but Christ lives in me. The life I live in the body, I live by faith in the Son of God, who loved me and gave himself for me" (Galatians 2:20). The surrendering of your ego to conform to that of Christ can be empowering. Paul's life exemplifies this.

Earlier, we have touched on the prescription St. Paul had for the transformation of your mind to attain empowerment and freedom. Paul asked you to put to death your "old man", those desires of the flesh that worked against the Spirit, and be "renewed in our mind" through faith in Christ (Romans 12:2; Ephesians 4:20-24). It is a willful act that requires daily effort as suggested by Paul's statement, "I die daily" (1 Corinthians 15:31). Paul didn't physically die when he said this. But his effort to imitate Christ means he had to forego the desires of the flesh on a daily basis. Just as Paul felt empowered by faith in Christ (Philippians 4:13), the mind of Christ in you, too, can help you accomplish this.

- Your body is the temple of God. Keep it clean and healthy. If you firmly believed that you body now belongs to God, as the owner of a priceless crystal, you will be motivated to keep it safe from harm, sickness, addictive drugs and substances, as well as moral and ethical lapses. This requires a transformation of values. And it is part of the process of change when you're "in Christ", as you yield your desires, and adopt God's value. Read the books of the New Testament, particularly St. Paul's letters to the Romans, Ephesians, Galatians, etc. They clearly explicated this concept and process.

- You are God's workmanship in Christ.
  As Daniel's life exemplifies, your life can be transformed to become an effective instrument of God. It means believing God has a purpose for you. God, the greatest architect, can sculpt your life into a beautiful art piece. Paul reminds us, "For we are God's workmanship, created in Christ Jesus to do good works, which God prepared in advance for us to do" (Ephesians 2:10).

STEP 4. TAKING CONCRETE ACTION TO CHANGE INDIVIDUALLY AND COLLECTIVELY.

Christ's metaphor of the eyes enlightening the whole body may apply to changes at both the individual and corporate level. Daniel's life is a shining example of an individually changed life.

In the June 11, 2012 *TIME* Magazine article entitled, "Does God Want You to be Thin?" authors Jeffrey Kluger and Elizabeth Dias reported that the Bible passage, "Daniel resolved not to defile himself with the royal food and wine", inspired Rick Warren's congregation devise a Daniel's Plan for healthier style of living. The Daniel Plan consisted of adherence to sound medical advice for overall health status including measurements, diet, exercise, sleep, avoidance of harmful substance, centering thoughts based on biblical passages, group support, and relying on the Scriptures for encouragement and motivation. Warren's congregation shed a collective 260,000 pounds. Warren himself has lost 55 lbs., with 35 more to go. Such is the power of saying no on a corporate level.

CONCLUSION

Psychospirituality can motivate you to look within yourself, to align your conscious and unconscious mind and your ego ideal with Christ's mind. It can propel you and your group to embark on a course of healthier living, achieving your goal to be Christ-like, and empower you to say no to harm and yes to God.

Chapter 13. KEY POINTS

1.   The power to say no stem from an alignment of your conscious and unconscious mind, a coming together of your id (impulses), ego, and ego ideal with the mind of Christ. It puts you on a path to attain a Christ-like nature, unencumbered by neurotic conflicts. It is a conscious act backed by your unconscious mind, seeking to know and to adopt the teaching and example of Christ.

2.   This state of mind is characterized by the following biblical verses reflecting a transformation of values:

   a.   Christ lives in you. Aligning your ego and ego ideals with that of Christ.

   b.   Your body is the temple of God. Keep it clean and holy

   c.   You are God's workmanship in Christ. Be an effective instrument for God.

3.   Daniel's life is a shining example of an individually empowered him.

4.   At a corporate level, Rick Warren's church and their Daniel Plan showed how the church can likewise be empowered to promote living with healthier life style.

CHAPTER 14

The Power Of Dream:
Knowing Your True Friend

I will pour out my Spirit on all people…and your old men will
dream dreams, your young men will see visions (Joel 2:28)

D ream is an outstanding feature of the book of Daniel.
In this chapter, you will learn how dream can empower
your life. After a brief discussion on the history of dream
research, I shall share a dream from my dream journal and its analysis
to illustrate dream's empowering effect.

INTRODUCTION

We spent 1/3 of our time in sleep, and we dreamed typically
20–25% of total sleep, about 90–120 minutes of a night's sleep.
Obviously, dream serves certain functions. But what are dreams?
What functions do they serve?

Men have dreamed since antiquity. Husser (1999) in her book,
Dreams and Dream Narrative in the Biblical World, pointed out that
ancient Egyptians and Greeks believed dreams were supernatural

events, and dreams held curative power.[25] In ancient Egypt and Mesopotamia, everyday dreams were meticulously documented (pp. 17-19).

Plato (c. 428-348 B.C.) was interested in the influences of dreams on a person's mental and physical life, and believed that dream messages could signal how a person should lead his or her life. (19)

Aristotle (384-322 B.C.) regarded dreams were related to memories of the dreamer's working day. His idea that metaphor was crucial in dream analysis formed the basis of modern dream interpretation.

In Roman times, Artimedorus of Daldis (150 A.D.) in *Oneirocriticon* ("*The Interpretation of Dreams*") (22) considered dreams rooted in the dreamer's waking world. Interpretation of dream should consider the dreamer's social status, place of work, physical and mental conditions. Artimedorus distinguished two types of dreams:
1.   Dreams that were influenced by natural phenomena--products of the body, its state of the organs or of its desires and fears that had no revelatory function.

2.   Dreams that were of divinatory nature.[26]

Artimedorous also distinguished two types of dream according to its ease of interpretation:
1.   *Theoromatic* dreams that were immediately comprehensible;

2.   *Allegorical* dreams that needed interpretation. (23)

Artimedorus's distinction between *theoromatic* and *allegorical* dreams formed the basis for modern historical critics to define two general types of dreams that are distinguishable one from the other by virtue of their respective literary form:
1.   *Message–dream* (23): This was characterized by the sudden appearance in a dream of a divinity or of someone who communicated a clear message that was unmistakably

intelligible to the sleeper. Auditory perceptions dominated this kind of dream. The visual element was usually limited to a description of the figure that conveyed the dream. The dreamer may enter a dialogue with the figure that appeared in the dream. Joseph's dream in the New Testament period to take Mary and Jesus to Egypt to escape Nero's harm is an example of this type of dream.

2. *Allegorical or symbolic dream* (23). This type of dream contained messages presumably from gods that were encoded in images, pictures, and events, whose significance escaped the dreamer. Visual perception was prominent. The meaning of the dream was not intelligible to the dreamer and required the interpretation by a third party.[27] Nebuchadnezzar's dream of the big stature is an example.

BIBLICAL PERSPECTIVE ON DREAM

In the biblical world, dream had long been regarded as a vehicle for the conveyance of God's will and messages. Parker (1985), in *Dream and Spirituality*, pointed out that there are more than 250 references to the subject in the Bible.[28] The verb "to dream" in the Old Testament is *harlam*...which means to make whole or healthy.

Dreams played prominent roles in divine guidance and protection for the Patriarchs.

(a) *Warning dream*

• When Abimelech, king of Gerar, unknowingly took Abraham's wife Sarah to be his wife, the Lord revealed in a dream to warn him that he would die if he touched Sarah, thus sparing Abraham disgrace. Not only was Sarah returned to Abraham, the clarification of Sarah's situation moved Abimelech to bestow land, sheep, cattle, and slaves for Abraham, and granted Abraham a safe refuge in the land of Abimelech (Genesis 20:3-7).

(b) *Predictive dream*

- At Bethel, God in a dream revealed to Jacob that he will be blessed, his descendants will be given the land on which he was lying and they will spread to all corners of the earth (Genesis 28).
- Joseph's ability to interpret Pharaoh's dreams convinced Pharaoh to store up grains during the seven years of good harvest in preparation for famine. Pharaoh put him in charge of his project. In turn, Joseph eventually helped his family escaped famine (Genesis 40-41).
- While scouting the forces of the Medianites, Gideon and his servant Purah overheard a Medianite soldier's dream that indicated to Gideon to attack the Medianites (Judges 7:13-15). Gideon acted on it and prevailed against the Medianites.

(c) *Reconciliatory dream*
- Through dream Jacob was reconciled with Laban, his father-in-law, at Gilead (Genesis 31:10-13).

(d) *Wish-fulfilling dream*
- At Gibeon, the Lord appeared to Solomon in a dream at night to grant his wish. Solomon asked for a discerning heart to govern his people and to distinguish right from wrong. This pleased the Lord in that he did not ask for long life, wealth, or death for his enemies. God not only granted him wisdom to govern, but also riches, honor and a long life (I Kings 3).

(e) *Guidance dream*
In New Testament time, three guidance dreams were recorded regarding Joseph, Mary, and the infant Jesus:
- Joseph was contemplating of quietly divorcing Mary when he found out that Mary was pregnant before they were married. The Lord appeared to Joseph in a dream to take

Mary home as his wife, because what was conceived in her was from the Holy Spirit. She was to give birth to a son and Joseph was to name him Jesus, because he will save his people from their sins (Matthews 1:18).

- The Lord again appeared to Joseph in a dream to take Jesus and Mary to Egypt because King Herod was plotting to kill the infant Jesus (Matthews 2:13).

- After Herod's death, an angel of the Lord appeared in a dream to Joseph in Egypt to return to the land of Israel with his family (Matthew 2:19).

CONTEMPORARY STUDY OF DREAM AND DREAMING

Freud, Jung and other analysts spurred renewed interest to understand the nature of dream and its use as a therapeutic tool. Aserinky and Kleitman[29], and Dement and Wolpert[30], in the 1950s, observed that dreams took place primarily during a distinctive electrophysiological phase of sleep on brain (EEG) tracing called the rapid eye movement (REM) stage. This provided a tool to examine the biological substrate of dream and dreaming in relation to its content. A person can now be awakened during the REM stage of sleep and asked to report his or her dream. The dream can then be correlated with EEG tracing and other events of the day. Research has shown that dream stimuli most likely originated from deep pontine and the midbrain reticular activating circuit and nuclei, and traveled upward to arouse multiple forebrain structures.[31] The connection with the frontal, parietal, occipital and limbic brain structure instigated the goal-seeking behavior, the brain's wanting, wishing command center.[32,33]

FUNCTIONS OF DREAM AND DREAMING

Despite the recent prodigious output of researches on dream and dreaming, there is as yet no consensual scientific opinion on the functions of dream. Here are a few opinions expressed by various authors:

- Dream is the royal road to the unconscious. (Freud).
- Dream tells a story, written in symbolic language... Dream expresses the inner experience of a person. (Erich Fromm)[34]
- All dreams are projections of the dreamer's own world; and of the ways in which the dreamer wished to lead his or her life. Dreams reflect unresolved personal and emotional issues not yet dealt with in waking life. (Fritz Perls, gestalt therapist).
- Dreaming (REM sleep) is to allow the brain to sift through that day's events, process any negative emotion attached to them, and then strip it away from the memories. Dreaming is likened to the process to applying a "nocturnal soothing balm" (Matthew Walker, University of California's Berkeley's Sleep and Neuroimaging lab).

Although various researchers may differ on the significance of dreams, all can agree that the dream experience is real. Dream and dreaming are subjective experiences that vary among individuals. Dream involves images and metaphors that sometimes made sense and sometimes not. It fades rapidly upon awakening. And it may stir strong emotion. Sometimes the meaning of the dream is obvious, but many times the meaning lies hidden from consciousness. You intuitively sense that the logic of dreaming, in contrast to that of the waking life, is different. Like a foreign musical composition, dream seems to have a logic, cadence, and meaning of its own.

DREAM CAN BE UNDERSTOOD

Freud and Jung greatly contributed to our understanding of dream and dreaming. Freud's (1856-1939) *Interpretation of Dream*[35] described how the human mind created the dream experience through the dream work mechanism. Freud considered dream as a sort of substitute for thought processes, full of meaning and emotion, at which he arrived after the completion of analysis.[36] He maintained that the unconscious contained the repository of repressed thoughts, feelings, and memories that formed the bulk of latent dream content. Through the process of free association, you can trace the dream material from the "manifest content" to the "latent", thus, making the unconscious, conscious. With new insight gained about yourself, you can then decide what to do with the newly discovered material.

Carl Jung, a contemporary of Freud, was a master of self-analysis. He spent his whole life analyzing his dreams to gain self-understanding. He analyzed in depth even his earliest childhood memories and brought them to bear upon his current manifest dream content. The result made him a person who had achieved tremendous insight into his innermost character, even his inner "gods and demons." He even concretized his dream symbols and unconscious in a stone structure to reflect his innermost thought, and of the knowledge he had acquired. The stone tower he built, the Bollingen house, became his "confession of faith in stone."[37]

Jung observed that the psyche spontaneously produces images with a religious content.[38] Jung wrote of his personal experience of God, "At that time I realized that God—for me, at least—was one of the most immediate experiences"[39] Jung considered understanding dream as pathways to personal and spiritual growth.

In addition to psychoanalysis, hypnosis and meditation are other techniques that can also access the unconscious.

DREAM INTERPRETATION TECHNIQUE

"*On Dream*", Freud gave an example of a short dream he analyzed himself, and laid bare the technique of free-association as follow:

1. Divide the dream into its element and find the association attaching to each of these fragments separately (20);

2. Report whatever occurs to mind without any exception to the analyst (or to oneself);

3. Find the connection of psychical materials generated [latent content] with the element of the manifest content under consideration. (24)

My colleague, Loma Flowers, M.D. and her collaborator, Gayle Delaney, PhD, had established the Delaney and Flowers Dream Center in San Francisco. You can access the simple technique of brief dream recording and interpretation at their Website, (http://www.gdelaney.com).

SAMPLE DREAM AND ITS INTERPRETATION FROM MY DREAM JOURNAL

Let me share with you the application of dream analysis to achieve self-realization and insight. This dream was taken from my dream journal. Since I have had psychoanalytic experience, and am familiar with the free association technique, in the interest of brevity, I have left out the trend and details of associative thoughts to arrive at the meaning of the dream. Below is my dream narrative, with syntax and grammar of sentences suspended, just as I jotted it down.

Title of Dream: Dr. Deng Pan

Day Notes: Deng Pan's name popped into my dream. He's a post-doc research fellow from China who used to attend our Christian Evangelistic Fellowship at UC Berkeley. I do not know him well. Recently, I have been in contact with the program committee of the Northern California Psychiatric Society to invite Dr. Ding of China to present in our annual meeting. Yesterday, I have had conversation yesterday with Dr. Paul Yang, a psychiatric colleague, regarding my current research interest in dreams, and my writing on Daniel. Also yesterday, I was thrilled that the San Francisco Giants defeated the Phillies (6 to 5) to capture the Western Conference title. I have also been researching the Gospel of John 17, in preparation for a sermon.

The Dream: I was interviewing for a research position at Bedford VA Hospital at Bedford, Massachusetts, where I worked for 23 years.

Met Dr. Deng Pan, a neurologist recently recruited from Taiwan to be the hospital director. Dr. Pan was engaged in basic research, had his own grant, and I was impressed. Bedford had also been engaged in basic neurological research.

Since Dr. Pan was new to the USA, I invited him to tour our house in Newton, Massachusetts. Willy, my best friend joined us in the tour. It was late for Willy, so we had to rush through viewing the different rooms. We started on the first floor, then the second. Suddenly, Elder Mrs. Co Guat Hua from the United Evangelical Church in Manila joined us. She kept asking where the outside corridor would lead. There was an outside door, I told her, and sometimes we passed through it. Then we reached the third floor with a ladder leading to the roof, just like the ladder to the roof of our rented house where our family used to live at Sanchez Extension Street, in Manila. It was raining, and Mrs. Co was interested in viewing the different roofs of different buildings. I dissuaded her because of the rain.

Then we came down. Elder Co, Willy and I started reminiscing about various people we met when we were young. I told them that once during the Lord's Supper at church, with eyes closed, images of the younger days appeared in my mind. We all laughed.

We went back to viewing the rooms on the lower floor. The house was full of people--brothers and sisters from church and friends, including Wei-Ming, my wife's half-brother. I introduced many friends to Dr. Pan, including one from Taiwan, who knew him. Willy had to leave at around 10:00 pm. It was already around 10:30 so we had to rush through viewing the various rooms, and missed some. On re-entering the house, I told Dr. Pan that the best room was on the right side of the house where my office was located. Earlier, he was introduced to my parents who were glad to see him. He said his surname was "Deng", like the Deng in Deng Pang Lin, a member of our Lexington Chinese Bible Church of Greater Boston, who recently passed away. End of dream.

Self-analysis: My free association led me to the recall of the following meanings:

a.   Dr. Deng Pan personifies my Chinese cultural roots, and my recent contact and experience with Dr. Ding in China, who had invited me to present a lecture at his hospital. I had wished to reciprocate his invitation by inviting him to present at our Northern California Psychiatric Society's annual meeting. Dr. Pan's director position at Bedford VA Hospital represents my current wish and aspiration to be "recruited" to do some basic research (Bedford has done solid neurological brain research), and to be a "director." I have had a long desire to become a chairperson in a department of psychiatry, a position that had eluded me. Deng Pan Ling, a member of our Lexington Church's congregation, who died recently, reminded me that I am no longer young (I am 72 years old at the time of this writing) and that my time is limited. Thus, the name *Deng* is a condensation of several layers of meaning: my cultural root, my wish to do research, my desire to invite Dr. Ding, my wish to become a departmental chair, and a reminder of my time in life now.

b.   Bedford VA Hospital is where I spent 23 years taking care of veterans before I retired from the U.S. federal service. During my tenure at Bedford VA, I was most productive academically. I produced three books on Cross-Cultural Psychiatry. But I still wish to have a second chance to do basic science research.

c.   The Newton House with different rooms represents my personal and professional attainments at different stages of my life. The office at the right side of my house was where I began my private practice of psychiatry. At Newton, MA, my clinical identity evolved. The different stories of the house suggest that I have attained recognition at different stages of my professional career. But I still wish to go higher as indicated by the corridor on my third floor, and the ladder leading to the rooftop. But the rain, an event from above, stopped me. (Raindrops can become water that nourishes the body, soul, and spirit. It can also become torrents of water that inundates or overwhelms. The fact that raindrops came from "above" suggests a heavenly "gentle whisper" not to launch on project beyond what my current capacity will allow. It also reveals the conflict in my life's goals now).

d.   Both Willy and Elder Co represent my past in Manila. I used to chat with Willy and Romy (my other friend not appearing in the dream) for long hours at the rooftop of our house about Willy's adventure in his courtship. We also discussed our future life plans. At that time, my future appeared gloomy and pessimistic. Ten thirty (10:30 pm) means that it may be late in life to pursue basic research project now. I have been experiencing conflicting life's agenda and schedules in my desire to complete my study and writing on Daniel vs. acquiring a grant to do research on sudden cardiac death in the Philippines.

PsychoSpiritual Lesson: The dream confirmed my narcissistic wish of wanting to reach an even higher level of professional attainment at this stage of my life, and the conflict that I have been experiencing. To do both at the same time may be unrealistic. My wish to pursue basic science research has become a distraction from finishing my writing on Daniel. In the context of my belief as a Christian at this stage of my life, I feel that my dream is a "gentle whisper" from the Holy Spirit to prioritize my work. Armed with the new insight from my dream, I re-evaluated and re-focused my priority on what is realistic, and decided to postpone my research project in sudden cardiac death. (See also chapter 18)

Thus, in one dream, it summarizes my life's past and current aspirations, conflicts, shortcomings, and accomplishments. The dream helps me to prioritize my current agenda. By aligning my unconscious and conscious motives, the dream honestly tells me, as no other close friends could, various factors that I must seriously consider in making important decisions at this stage of my life, and how to resolve my conflict. This is the power of dream. It gives you insight that is rarely accessible from any other source. Let dream be your true friend.

> Go confidently in the direction of your dreams!
> --Henry David Thoreau

Chapter 14. KEY POINTS

- Ancient Middle Eastern people took their dream seriously and had developed a system of classifying and analyzing dream.
- Dreams that were mundane were differentiated from dreams that had prophetic or oracular significance.
- The Bible had long regarded dream and vision as God's way of communicating with men.
- Discovery of a high frequency of dreaming during the REM stage of sleep EEG initiated research to correlate dream content with brain wave activities.
- Dreams can be understood and interpreted through free associative technique, meditation, and hypnosis.
- Dream is the "royal road to the unconscious mind."
- Dreams, properly interpreted, can empower by providing insights to promote emotional and spiritual growth, and can guide life's decision.

CHAPTER 15

The Power Of Belief: Trusting God And Your Motivational System

Therefore everyone who hears these words of mine [Christ,
on Sermon on the Mount], and put them into practice
is like a wise man who built his house on the rock
(Matthew 7:24)

YOUR BRAIN IS A SPIRITUAL BRAIN

Your brain is not just a supercomputer, it is a "spiritual brain."
Harvard neuropathologist, Paul Yakovlev, M.D. proposed
a model of the central nervous system that is an integral
part of a whole biosphere of living matters that constitutes a uni-
tary dynamic system.[40] Yakovlev noted that during embryonic development of the central nervous system, the direction of movement
spreads from center out, from behind forward, and from simplicity
to specialization, creating three distinct anatomic zones, with each
zone serving particular functions.

1. An innermost, "median" zone that regulates "visceral
motility", including basic cellular metabolism, respiration,

circulation, peristalsis, secretion, excretions, etc., whose activity is largely confined within the body. This zone basically promotes the instinctual ability of the organism to survive, as in the continuous beating of the heart despite brain death.

2.   An intermediate, "paralimbic" zone that regulates "motility of an outward expression of internal states." This includes the verbal and non-verbal communication of our emotional states. This zone prepares human organism to relate to the outer world, but "does not, per se, effect changes in the world around it."

3.   An outer or "supralimbic" zone that regulates "motility of effectuation." This zone creates changes in the world through producing works that impact on the environment. This zone, including the frontal cortex, is responsible for the highest level of human achievements.

Extending Yakovlev's model, activity of the "supralimbic" zone is what enabled NASA to land Neil Armstrong on the moon, and the Curiosity module on Mars. The supralimbic zone also enabled us to create culture, that third intervening environment between our biological endowment and the natural world we live in.[41] This zone allowed you to appreciate the awesomeness of the universe, beauty, inference about the creator, and to pray. In short, your ability to relate to the spiritual world is dependent on the integrity and activities of your supralimbic zone.

Your brain is hard-wired to believe until proven otherwise

Advances in technological tools, including the functional MRI, have enabled scientists to identify and map more closely areas in our brain that engaged in higher-level mental activity so that now, we are beginning to appreciate what Oliver Sacks and Joy Hirsch, editorialized, as the "Neurology of Belief."[42]

In a study of 14 adults to differentiate belief, disbelief, and uncertainty at the level of the brain, Harris, Sheth, and Cohen (2008) found that belief (accepting a proposition as "true"), disbelief ("untrue"), and uncertainty ("undecidable") activated different areas of prefrontal cortex (that part of the brain in front of your head) as well as parts of the limbic system (your emotional brain), and basal ganglia (part of the brain's motivational system and motor control) in all three cases. Brain areas most engaged in belief included the ventral medial prefrontal cortex, specifically the gyrus rectus and orbitomedial gyrus. These areas are known for connection to emotional associations with reward contingencies. In contrast, disbelief tended to engage the inferior frontal gyrus, the anterior insula, superior parietal lobule, and dorsal cingulate gyrus. These dorsal structures are known for their roles in executive functions and decision-making. Insula is thought to be involved in reactions to pain and disgust.[43]

The reaction time it took to generate a response in belief was significantly faster compared to that of disbelief and uncertainty.[40]

These data suggested that a proposition accepted as true tended to be pleasant and rewarding. Proposition rejected as untrue took more time to arrive at, and tended to be more unpleasant.

The authors suggested that the faster reaction time in belief tended to support Spinoza's conjecture that the "mere comprehension of a statement entails the tacit acceptance of its being true, an almost reflexive, if conditional assent, to be followed by more deliberative assessment and judgment." (143) Human brains, it seems, are hard-wired to accept appearances as reality until they prove otherwise, and the authors addressed the neural correlates of belief, disbelief, and uncertainty, as different state of mind.

RELIGIOUS BELIEF MAY INVOLVE DIFFERENT BRAIN CIRCUITRY

In a subsequent study, Harris et al. (2009)[44] devised another experiment to address two related questions: 1) What brain structures underlie belief (judgments of "true") and disbelief (judgments of "false") when religious propositions were introduced? 2) Whether religious believers and nonbelievers differ in how they evaluate statements of facts.

Harris et al.'s second experiment presented written statements of religious and nonreligious proposition to 15 committed Christians and 15 nonbelievers while they were in the functional MRI scanner. The statements were designed to produce a clear "true" or "false" answer, such as religious statement, "Jesus Christ really performed the miracles attributed to him in the Bible", or a nonreligious statement, "Alexander the Great was a very famous military leader." Brain signal changes were measured as they evaluated the truth and falsity of religious and nonreligious propositions and the results were compared with baseline.

The results showed for both groups and in both categories of statements, belief activated strong signal in the ventromedial prefrontal cortex, a finding that duplicated similar result from his previous study (Harris et al., 2008). This brain area is thought to be related to self-representation, emotional association, reward, and goal-directed behavior. Earlier, Sacks and Hirsch (2008) asked whether all reactions of assent or acceptance (or belief) are neurophysiologically identical, regardless of propositional judgments made in the highly charged realm of ethical or religious issues, or in the seemingly neutral realm of arithmetical statement. The fact that Harris et al. found essentially the same signal maps for belief in both groups, and on both categories of content (emotionally charged and emotionally neutral arithmetical items), is another step that suggests belief and disbelief appeared to involve separate cognitive processes, irrespective of the content of the stimuli. This finding, if further duplicated, would be a fascinating discovery.

Moreover, responses to religious statements compared to non-religious ones activated a wide range of signal throughout the brain, including the precuneus, anterior cingulate, insula, ventral striatum, and posterior medial cortex. These brain areas are associated with perception of pain in oneself and others, emotional processing and reward, cognitive planning, conflict resolution, and self-referential tasks. The involvement of these brain structures would support Harris et al.'s notion that "the evaluation of religious statements would more fully engage regions of brain responsive to emotional salience, both positive and negative." Nonreligious statements seem to register greater signals in the left hemispheric networks, including the hippocampus, the parahippocampal gyrus, middle temporal gyrus, temporal pole and retrosplenial cortex. These brain areas are well known for memory tasks, including its retrieval. This seemed to imply that evaluation of nonreligious statement of facts evoked less emotional salience.

An interesting corollary finding involved a subset of statements that run counter to Christian doctrine and are considered blasphemous by believers (e.g., "The Biblical god is a myth"). Both believers and nonbelievers registered strong signals in several brain regions, including the ventral striatum, para-cingulate gyrus, middle frontal gyrus, the frontal poles, and inferior parietal cortex. These regions showed greater signal when both Christians rejected the statements contrary to their doctrine, and nonbelievers affirmed the truth of those same statements. It seemed that when nonbelievers made assertion that explicitly negate religious doctrine, and when Christians rejected the same statements as false, both groups seemed to take special pleasure in doing so.

The finding of response time to statements also differed for both groups. The response times were significantly longer for false, compared to true responses, and also for religious, compared with nonreligious statements. While both groups were quicker to respond "true" to "false" on both categories of stimuli, the effect of truth was especially pronounced for nonbelievers when responding to religious statements. The longer response time for religious propositions for both groups would support Harris et al.'s conjecture that "both groups experienced greater cognitive conflict and uncertainty while evaluating religious statements."

The fact that belief, in general, and religious belief, specifically, involved deep structures of the brain linked with emotional salience may well explain why religious sentiments remain a powerful feature of human behavior. Harris et al., quoting Boyer (2001, 2003), suggested that:

> Human have cognitive templates for religious ideas that run deeper than culture... people do not accept implausible religious doctrines because they have relaxed their standard of rationality; they relax their standard of rationality because certain doctrines fit their "inference machinery" in such a way to seem credible. And what religious propositions may lack in plausibility they made up for in the degree to which they are memorable, emotionally salient, and socially consequential; all of these properties are a product of our cognitive architecture, and most of this architecture is not consciously accessible." (3)

Belief is motivating because thoughts incorporated into your "personal religion" can become the "explanatory model" of your existence and your "total way of life."

HOW DOES BELIEF MOTIVATE AND EMPOWER?

You have noted that belief engaged the ventral/medial prefrontal cortex that has strong connections to the limbic and basal ganglia areas of brain, areas that have strong emotional and motivational salience.

Monique Ernst, Daniel Pine and Michael Hardin (2006) of the U.S. National Institute of Mental Health wanted to understand the brain structures that underlie adolescence's risk-taking behavior.

Based on a cognitive science approach, they proposed a "Triadic" model to explain adolescent's typical and atypical behavior.[45] What they proposed, interestingly, also involved the medial/ventral pre-frontal cortex, brain area that Harris et al. found to be involved in response to beliefs. The Triadic model proposed:

1. A reward system, the nucleus accumbens, that is rich in dopamine, the "reward" neuro-transmitter;

2. An avoidant system, the amygdala; and,

3. A supervisory system, the medial/ventral prefrontal cortex.

It seemed that adolescents who engaged in thrill-seeking cocaine risk-taking behavior may have a propensity to have "a strong reward system, a weak harm-avoidant system, and/or an inefficient supervisory system" (Ernst et al., 2006). Thus, an imbalance in this tri-partite system may lead to harmful consequences.

On the contrary, a balanced "triadic" system seemed to promote more typical or normative behavior by allowing a more careful assessment of what is good for you. Since "belief" engages the medial/ventral prefrontal cortex, the "supervisory" part of this triadic system, it stands to reason that if "belief" is summoned to participate in the assessment and judgment of behavior, belief could provide important input and motivation.

This may have relevance to what William James, M.D., referred to as the "religious sentiment" that can powerfully motivate human behavior (See Appendix, Conceptual Issue). James had called our attention to the motivating effect of religious beliefs. He defined religion as "feelings, acts, and experiences of individual men…as they apprehend themselves in relation to whatever they may consider the divine."

James asserted that as a system of thoughts, religion could stir up "strong sentiments that are as real as any concretized experience that our sensory systems could evoke." When an entity is considered godlike, it impels us to action; therefore, becomes empowering, i.e., strong motivator for action (See Appendix). Because religious ideas could stir up strong sentiments, James regarded religion as "man's total reaction to life."

CONCLUSION

The middle/lower (medial/ventral) part of your frontal lobe is most likely involved in psycho-spiritual experience. This part of the brain has a rich connection with the reward center (nucleus accumbens), and emotional circuit (the limbic system) to give your thoughts and actions the emotional valence to act.

Belief can be motivating because it engages regions of the brain that are memorable, emotionally salient, and socially consequential. We are hard-wired to believe propositions until they prove otherwise. The important question is not so much whether you could believe or not, but what you choose to believe in.

ALBERT C. GAW, M.D.

Chapter 15. KEY POINTS

1.   Your brain is a spiritual brain. The architecture of the brain is constructed with the ability to abstract and relate to "spiritual matters."

2.   Your brain is hard-wired to belief until proven otherwise.

3.   Religious belief may involve different brain circuitry.

4.   Belief is motivating because thoughts incorporated into your "personal religion" can become the "explanatory model" of your existence, and your "total way of life."

5.   The middle/lower (medial/ventral) part of your frontal lobe is most likely involved in psychospiritual experience. This part of the brain has a rich connection with the reward center (nucleus accumbens), and emotional circuit (the limbic system) to give your thoughts and actions the emotional valence to act.

6.   A triadic model involving the medial/ventral frontal cortex, the amygdala, and nucleus accumbens has been proposed to explain adolescent typical and atypical behavior. An imbalance in this equilibrium is believed to explain adolescence risk-taking behavior. Belief, through its influence on the ventral/medial prefrontal cortex, could contribute to the balancing of this equilibrium.

7.   The critical question is not to believe, but *what* you choose to believe in.

CHAPTER 16

The Power Of Humility: Being Esteemed By Man And God

Daniel, you who are highly esteemed…do not be afraid. Since
the first day that you set your mind to gain understanding and
to humble yourself before your God, your words were heard,
and I have come in response to them (Daniel 10:11-12)

INTRODUCTION

D aniel's book emphasizes stories of people seized with pride
and their downfall. At the same time, the lesson of humility exemplified by Daniel's actions, earned him the esteem
of man and God (Daniel 10:11-12). To be successful, you have to
learn to be humble. Humility seemed to be the channel through
which blessings flow.

The following characters in the Book of Daniel prominently
exemplified the theme of pride and its consequence.
1. Nebuchadnezzar's dream of the huge stature with Babylon
and him as the golden head of the stature (chapter 2).

2. Nebuchadnezzar acted out his dream by building 90 feet high and 9 feet wide gold stature of him, and demanded all his subjects pray to the idol (chapter 3).

3. Nebuchadnezzar boasted his empire and power and his mind suddenly was turned into that of an animal (chapter 4).

4. Belshazzar's arrogant display and use of the holy vessels taken from Jerusalem temple, and then saw the vision of the "hand-writing" on the palace's wall. He was subsequently assassinated and the Babylon empire came to an end. (chapter 5).

5. Persian King Darius I succumbed to the trick of his counselors in issuing an edict to pray only to him for 30 days, and ended sending Daniel, his beloved minister, to the lions' den (chapter 6).

6. Antiochus Epiphanes IV appeared as the "little horn" that grew big in Daniel's vision of the Goat and Ram (chapter 8).

7. The antichrist's boasting and assumption of power during end time (chapters 7, 11).

WHAT IS PRIDE?

Wikipedia considered "pride (Latin, *superbia*), or hubris (Greek), the original and most serious of the seven deadly sins, and the source of the others. Pride is identified as a desire to be more important or attractive than others, failing to acknowledge the good work of others, and excessive love of self (especially holding self out of proper position toward God). Dante's definition was 'love of self perverted to hatred and contempt for one's neighbour.' In perhaps the best-known example, the story of Lucifer, pride (his desire to compete with God) was what caused his fall from Heaven, and his resultant transformation into Satan" (en.wikipedia.org/wiki/Seven_deadly_sins).

The American Heritage Dictionary (1976, p.1039) defined pride as:

1.   A sense of one's own proper dignity or value, or self-respect.

2.   Pleasure or satisfaction taken in one's work, achievement or possessions.

3.   An exceedingly high opinion of oneself, conceit, or arrogance.

Pride in the first two instances implies a healthy aspect of your personality, when your feeling is backed up with achievements or actions. The feeling of a "glow" after a successful performance by a vocalist or an orchestral conductor; the pride of an author signing his or her book, are natural reactions to a sense of accomplishments earned after hard works. That feeling of pride is natural. In fact, it is conducive to the development of self-esteem and self-respect. On the other hand, an exceedingly high opinion of oneself, conceit, or arrogance as demonstrated by Nebuchadnezzar and Belshazzar, could become maladaptive and lead to one's downfall. No wonder in Christian ethics, pride was listed as a cardinal sin. Adam and Eve sinned because of their pride to become co-equal with God, their creator.

Thus, pride ranges from shades of normal adaptive feelings to grossly maladaptive grandiosity. Proverbs cautioned against pride.
- When pride comes, then comes disgrace, but with humility comes wisdom (Proverbs 11:2).
- Pride only breeds quarrel, but wisdom is found in those who takes advice (Proverbs 13:10).

ALBERT C. GAW, M.D.

- Pride goes before destruction, a haughty spirit before a fall (Proverbs 16:18).
- A man's pride brings him low, but a man of lowly spirit gains honor (Proverbs 29:23).

Pride or arrogance can intrude and interfere on smooth interpersonal relation. It can blind arrogant persons from receiving sound advice and dooms them to their own grandiose thinking and ways.

If the shade of pride crosses over to become entrenched personality pattern it becomes pathological. Psychoanalyst calls this "narcissism", implying an excessive admiration of oneself. In psychoanalysis, narcissism is "an arresting of development at, or a regression to, an infantile stage of development in which one's own body is the object of erotic interest." (The American Heritage Dictionary 1976, p. 872). The term is borrowed from Greek Mythology in which Narcissus, a youth who, having spurned the love of Echo, pined away in love for his own image in a pool of water and was transformed into a flower that bears his name (American Heritage Dictionary 1976, p. 872). Both King Nebuchadnezzar and Belshazzar exhibited narcissistic behaviors. In Genesis 37, Joseph's two dreams also revealed his narcissism:

- Joseph's dreamed of binding sheaves of grain out in the filed when suddenly his sheaf rose and stood upright, while his brothers' sheaves gathered around his and bowed down to it. He told his brothers his dream and they said to him, "Do you intent to reign over us? Will you actually rule us? And they hated him all the more because of his dream and what he said (Genesis 37:5-8).

Joseph had a second dream, "…this time the sun and the moon and eleven stars were bowing down to me" (Genesis 37:9). When he told his father as well as his brothers his dream, his father rebuked him, "What is this dream you had? Will you and your mother and I and your brothers actually come and bow down to the ground before you?" His brothers were jealous of him, but his father kept the matter in mind (Genesis 37:10-11).

These two dreams revealed Joseph's inflated sense of self. He was arrogant and his unconscious revealed it to him in dreams. Yet, he naively told his brothers about the first dream, and to both his parents and brothers, the second. Every one in his family understood the meaning of the dreams. And these provoked intense jealousy and anger among his brothers that resulted in their determination to kill him. Were it not for divine intervention through his oldest brother Ruben's effort to spare his life, Joseph's fate and the story of the nation of Israel would have turned out to be very different.

NARCISSISTIC PERSONALITY DISORDER

Excessive deviation from the norm may lead to a more enduring pattern of abnormal behavior described as "narcissistic personality disorder." The Diagnostic and Statistical Manual of the American Psychiatric Association (DSM-IV-TR) spelled out the criteria.

1. A grandiose sense of self-importance (e.g., exaggerates achievements and talents, expects to be recognized as superior without commensurate achievements).

2. Pre-occupation with fantasies of unlimited success, power, brilliance, beauty or ideal love.

3. A belief that he or she is "special" and unique and can only be understood by, or should associate with, other special or high-status people (or institutions).

4. Requirement of excessive admiration.

5. A sense of entitlement, i.e., unreasonable expectations of especially favorable treatment or automatic compliance with his or her expectations.

6. Interpersonally exploitative, i.e., takes advantage of others to achieve his or her own ends.

7. Lack of empathy, is unwilling to recognize or identify with the feelings and needs of others.

8. Envious of others or a belief that others are envious of him or her.

9. Arrogant, haughty behaviors or attitudes.

In my opinion, both pride and narcissism may be intimately related to a reflexive unconscious over-compensation of one's low self-esteem, a feeling of being "small", "defective", or "inadequate." The idea is that in order to defend against such uncomfortable feelings, you unconsciously overcompensate by resorting to a behavioral pattern of over-inflating yourself.

HOW IS LOW-SELF-ESTEEM MANIFESTED?

People with low self-esteem feel "inadequate, defective, and small" when compared to others. Hence, they unconsciously strive to be number one all the time. You can easily spot such individuals. Here are some of my observations.

1. The "monopolizer" in group conversations.

2. Having the need to say the last word in discussion.

3. Constant use of the pronoun "I", and attributing success to oneself.

4. Other's success provokes intense jealously and anger.

5. Unconsciously always looking for events to blame oneself in order to justify one's "defects."

6. Launching projects to seek being number one.

7. Ignoring other's honest input, feeling hurt easily, and pulling away from people who don't agree with him/her.

8. Feeling isolated.

9. Prone to rationalization.

10. Dream of self-inflation or self–importance.

11. Abuse of power when in powerful social, political, or ecclesiastical position.

SLAYING THE DEMON

Confronting one's unconscious narcissism and low self-esteem is hard. You have to be convinced that you're better off to have a healthier self-esteem than to continue your old ways. It requires determination to change. If, after trying, you still feel unworthy, defective and small, then your issues may be more deeply engrained in your personality and may require professional help. Psychoanalytic oriented face-to-face psychotherapy, cognitive behavioral therapy and psychoanalysis are examples of procedure that can help. You can consult the experience of friends who had such treatment, or speak directly to a reputable therapist to consider whether these options are for you.

Psychospirituality, on the other hand, can help through motivation and revealing insights to change. Let's examine how Daniel did it.

- His judgment was guided by the scriptural precepts and religious beliefs.
    - ◦ Daniel resolved not to partake in the king's food and wine. He preferred the humble existence than partaking the king's morally "defiled" food and drink (chapter 1).
- He knew the scripture, and when convinced that God's moment had arrived, he acted decisively (chapter 9).
- He turned to God when his life, and that of his friends and the Babylonian wise men and their families were threatened (chapter 2, 6).
- He knew how to win friends and influence people. He won the friendship of his captor, Arioch, and the allegiance of his Babylonian colleagues by rescuing them from the king's wrath and execution.

- He surrounded himself with true friends and prayer partners, and promoted them into high positions when the opportunity knocked on the door.
- He praised God for rescuing him from the lions' mouth, and to his king for delivering him out of the lions' den.
- He knew the limit of his knowledge and how to turn to God for advice and interpretation of visions.
- He fasted and continued to seek God's revelation through dream and vision, knowing fully the emotional toll that will exact on him.
- He fervently prayed for the repentance of his people's sins, and petitioned God for the Jews to return to Judah from exile and rebuild Jerusalem.
- He sealed his prophecy as instructed by the angel Michael and patiently waited for his eventual heavenly reward, and expectation of bodily resurrection.

Daniel exercised exquisite diplomacy that stemmed from true humility. He gave credit where credit was due. If you are humble and learn to give credit to others, people will like you and trust you. John the Baptist was a powerful preacher and had many followers. But listen to him when he introduced Jesus, "I baptize with water, but among you stands one you do not know. He is the one who comes after me, the thongs of whose sandals I am not worthy to untie" (John 1:26-27).

CONCLUSION

Acknowledging other's contributions and credits requires sufficient self-esteem. A humble person uses words to pull other people in and acknowledges God for the source of one's blessings. Psychospirituality can motivate and empower you to seek humility, gain insights to slay your inner demons of narcissism, low self-esteem, and self-doubt.

Chapter 16: KEY POINTS

1. Both pride and narcissism can cause the downfall of man and nation.

2. Nebuchadnezzar's narcissism led to his mental illness.

3. Belshazzar's arrogance and sin led to his death and the demise of the Babylonian empire.

4. Narcissism can manifest in many ways, including the constant unconscious need seeking to be number one.

5. As Daniel had demonstrated, psychospirituality can help you slay the demon of pride and narcissism through insights gained from prayer, meditation, scripture reading, feedback from true friends, and acting upon them.

CHAPTER 17

The Power Of Prayer: Moving God's Heart

The prayer of a righteous man is powerful
and effective (James 5:16)

D aniel was a man of prayer (see chapter 6). He regularly prayed to God three times a day. He would rather suffer the consequence of death than forbidden to pray. He knew when to pray, how to pray, and the power of prayer. You can emulate Daniel's prayer life and be empowered.

Prayer can be said to be the oldest expression of human's desire to gain control of unpredictable and unexplained human events. This chapter will familiarize you on prayer from the Christian theological perspective. We shall not touch on published articles on the helpful effects of prayer and their controversies, though by themselves, they are interesting and important. We shall also not discuss the burgeoning body of research literature on the psychology of prayer, brain changes during state of prayer, intercessory prayers, and other related topics. From a psychospiritual viewpoint, I believe that it is irrelevant and impossible to discuss the power of prayer apart from a belief in God. The author of the book of Hebrews reminds us:

> Without faith, it is impossible to please God, because anyone who comes to him must believe that he exists and that he rewards those who earnestly seek him. (Hebrews 11:6)

Thus, in this context, we shall focus on biblical foundation of prayer, and how prayer can empower you.

Much has been written even about biblical prayers. Reviewing various sources of biblical commentaries on prayers, I like very much what Tim Chester has written on the *Message of Prayer* [46] because his thinking is consistent with my analysis of Daniel's psychospirituality. The following pages are my paraphrase of Chester's thoughts with my personal comments.

THE BIBLICAL FOUNDATION OF PRAYER

Prayer is the conversation of friends.

Tim Chester, in his book, *The Message of Prayer* (2003) laid out the biblical foundation of prayer. Prayer, Chester asserted, is the conversation of friends, God and man conversing as friend-to-friend. What a concept and privilege! Yet, for God's creatures to attain the status of friendship with God, the process involved creation and traversed human history.

1. [Prayer is God's Grace by inviting man to share in the fellowship of the Triune God]. Chester pointed out that the scriptural foundation of prayer started with "the riddle in creation" that occurred within the Triune God (Father, Son, and the Holy Spirit) to have man shared in this fellowship.

    > Let us make man in our image, in our likeness, and let them rule...in the image of God he created him; male and female he created him (Genesis 1:26-27).

The "us" suggested more than one person, the trinity of God--three persons, one godhead--each is both one with Him, and also distinct (p. 28). An intimate fellowship and communion existed within the Triune God. In His grace, God wanted human to share in this fellowship, so God created man and woman. And this fellowship served as the foundation of prayer.

> Creation is an act of grace in which God invites us to share the love of the Trinitarian life. God graciously purposes to have a relationship with people. (29)

> The riddle of creation is that God should desire to enter into a relationship with his creatures outside his Trinitarian being. And this riddle is the foundation of prayer--and not only of prayer but of human existence. (28)

2. [Adam and Eve sinned and sin broke this relationship]

Adam and Eve initially enjoyed a beautiful communal relationship with God at the Garden of Eden. However, they sinned, and sin broke this relationship. Instead of appearing before God, they hid from him in shame (Genesis 3:7). Eventually, they were driven out of the Garden of Eden and fellowship with God (Geneses 3:24).

3. [To restore this relationship, God began a movement to create a people that will belong to Him]

The first step to restore this relationship was the promise of a people that will belong to Him. (31) Yet, as Chester pointed out, from a position of "banished subjects" to "friendship with God" took a long journey through history. God chose Abraham to start this process of reconciliation.

God's promise to Abraham is that he will have offspring who will become a nation (Genesis 12:2)...not just a nation, but God's people. "I will establish my covenant as an everlasting covenant between me and you and your descendants after you for the generations to come, to be your God and the God of your descendants after you." (Genesis 17:7)

By the time of Exodus, Chester reminded us that Abraham descendants had become a great nation. But they were a people in slavery in Egypt and exiled from the promise land. God sent Moses to bring them out to the land promised to Abraham (Exodus 3:7,10) (31) and made this promise, "...I will take you as my own people, and I will be your God" (Exodus 6:7). Although the people did not listen to Moses because of their suffering from discouragement and cruel bondage, God did not force the Israelites to be obedient. Instead, through Moses, God showed His power and performed the miracles to convince Pharaoh to let His people leave Egypt (Exodus 6:9-10).

> Covenant partnership means that God cannot and does not use the divine prerogatives of power to reduce Israel's response to monotones of praise, submission, or silence. Such limitations on human response effectively eviscerate genuine covenant relationship, substituting instead enforced obedience and passive devotion. Covenant partnership also means that Israel cannot and does not withhold from God the full range of human experience. (Balentine. *Prayer in the Hebrew Bible*, 263) (31)

4. [The Mosaic Law was given to impart an understanding of this relationship]

At Sinai, God made a covenant with His people and gave them His law...["Observe them carefully, for this will show your wisdom and understanding to the nations, who will hear all about all these decrees and say, 'Surely this nation is a wise and understanding people.' 'What other nation is so great as to have their gods near them the way the Lord God is *near* us whenever we *pray* to him?'" (Deuteronomy 4:6-7)] Prayer drew God to His people! And the covenant showed them how.

•   [The Tabernacle was a symbol of God's dwelling with man]
At Sinai, Moses pitched tent some distance away from the camp where anyone inquiring of the Lord would go. Moses called it the "tent of meeting" (Exodus 33:7-8). Only Moses could enter the

tent. As Moses went in, the pillar of cloud would come down and stayed at the entrance, while the Lord spoke with Moses. The scripture attested, "The Lord would speak to Moses face to face, as a man speaks with his friend" (Exodus 33:11). Such was the intimacy of friendship between God and Moses. However, the people remained outside the tent.

Likewise, to experience the presence of God during their sojourn through the desert, the Israelites built tabernacles. "The instruction on the construction of the tabernacle and later the temple, captures this sense of presence and distance. The tabernacle represents God's presence with His people, but at the same time its various courts and the curtain in front of the Holy of Holies keep people from the consuming presence of God." (32)

"But the people at Sinai sinned against God by constructing a golden calf. God said he will give them the land but will not go with them (Exodus 33:3). Moses interceded for his people for 'there is no point in the prosperity in the land without the presence of God' (Exodus 33:15-16). The genius of Moses is to recognize that salvation is fellowship with God." (32)

- [Prayer made towards the Jerusalem temple was answered from heaven]

King David brought rest to the nation from its enemies. And, more significantly, God promised a 'house' [a dynasty] to David. David's son, Solomon, built a temple for God. In his prayer of dedication, Solomon asked God to be attentive to prayer offered towards the temple (1 Kings 8:29-51). But he realized that the God whom the heavens cannot contain does not live in something made by human hands. Solomon repeatedly implored God to "hear from heaven." Thus, the prayer made towards the temple was answered *from heaven*" (1 Kings 8:27-30) (33).

5.   [The Old Covenant gave way to the New]

Chester reminded us that because the people continued to turn away from God, by the time Psalm 137 was written, Jerusalem had fallen, the temple had been destroyed, and the people had been exiled to Babylon. This has happened not because God was unfaithful to His promise, but because the people were unfaithful (1 Kings 9:8-9) (33).

So all that is left is the bare promise of God and it is on this promise that the prophets reconstruct hope for God's people (34). The prophets then began to speak of a *new* covenant in which the law will be written on people's heart. And at the heart of this new covenant was once again the promise of a relationship.

> I will be their God,
> And they will be my people. (Jeremiah 31:33)

The post-exilic prophets also foretold of a new temple in a *new* Jerusalem that is far greater than the old one (Haggai 2:9; Zechariah 1-6). And this *new* Jerusalem will become the ultimate fulfillment of prayer (See section 10 below).

6.   [In Christ, the relationship between God and man was restored]

Over five hundred years after the fall of Jerusalem, the promise to Abraham was fulfilled in Jesus whose name means, Emmanuel, God with us (Matthew 1:23).

The gospel of John described the coming of Jesus, "The word became flesh and made his dwelling among us. We have seen his glory, the glory of the One and Only, who came from the Father, full of grace and truth" (John 1:14). "Made his dwellings" literally means, tabernacle, symbolizing God's presence (35). Jesus, in the Gospel of John, identified himself as the true temple…"Destroy this temple, and I will raise it again in three days [referring to his body, death and resurrection] (John 2:19-22). "Now God who cannot be approached is among his people in human form in the person of his Son" (35).

At the last supper, Jesus made a new covenant, constituting believers as the people of God. (John 15) (35). Through his death and resurrection, Jesus achieved God's saving grace to have a people who are His own. "The Son is going to bring us into a relationship with the Father" (35)... ["Father, just as you are in me and I am in you. May they [all believers] also be in us so that the world may believe that you have sent me. I have given them the glory that you gave me. May they be one as we are one. I in them and you in me" (John 17:22-23).]

As the gospel was preached to the gentiles, in a reversal of the covenant promise, through the hardening of the hearts of the Jews who were cast aside like broken olive branch, the believing gentiles, originally never a people of God, were now "grafted" into God's family tree and became co-heirs with Israel to receive the promise of God (Ephesian 3:6). Thus, both the Jews and gentile believers became a community of true believers and the church is the place where God dwells on earth (Ephesians 2:19-22) (35).

When Jesus died on the cross, the curtain in the temple was torn from top to bottom, symbolizing the barrier that had prevented direct access to the Holy of Holies in the temple was finally broken. (Mark 15:38) Now believers can freely come to the throne of grace. "The sin that once separated us from God has been cleansed through the sacrificial blood of Christ" (37). Our relationship with God is restored through Christ!

7.   [Prayer is the conversation of friends]

Jesus not only gave us access to God, he made us family. He invited us to call God 'Father', while he himself calls us his *friends*. (37) [...Shortly before his death he said to his disciples, "I no longer call you servants, because a servant does not know his master's business. Instead, I have called you *friends*, for everything that I learned from my Father I have made known to you" (John 15:15; 15:13-14)]. Jesus also mentioned:

> I tell you the truth, anyone who has faith in me will do what I have been doing. He will do even greater things than these, because I am going to the Father. And I will do whatever you ask me in my name, so that the Son may bring glory to the Father. You may ask for anything in my name, and I will do it (John 14:12-14)].

Thus, in Christ, we become God's friend. And through prayer in his name, Jesus promised that all our requests will be answered.

> In obedience the Christian is the servant, in faith he is the child, but in prayer, as the servant and the child, he is the friend of God, called to the side of God and at the side of God, living and ruling and reigning with Him. (K. Barth, *CD* III/3., p. 286) (37)

> God does not want us as objects, but as covenant partners, partners who can converse. He desires our conversation input, our spontaneous gratitude, our free concurrence, but also our patience or impatient questionings; and even our vehement protest is dearer to him than a silent, unconvinced acquiescence. (Hendrikus Berkhof cited in Stroup, *Reformed Reader*, vol. 2, p.231) (37)

Hence, prayer is an expression of the very heart of God's eternal plan to have a people who are His people, to know us and to be known by us (37).

8.   [The Ultimate fulfillment of prayer]

Chester called attention to John's vision in Revelation, "I saw the Holy City, the new Jerusalem, coming down out of heaven from God, prepared as a bride beautifully dressed for her husband. And I heard a loud voice from the throne saying, 'Now the dwelling of God is with men, and he will live with them. They will be his people, and God himself will be with them and be their God'" (Revelation 21:2-3).

The old covenant represented by Jerusalem was now fulfilled in the new creation. John did not see a temple in the city because the Lord God Almighty and the Lamb are its temple (Revelation 21:22). As Chester indicated, prayer is not the ultimate, but penultimate, a pointer to the day when we shall see God face to face even as we are truly known (1 Corinthians 13:12) (38).

IN SUMMARY

1. Prayer reflected God's grace inviting man to have fellowship with Him.

2. Adam's fall, and sin broke this relationship.

3. God initiated a movement to restore this relationship by creating a people for Himself through Abraham's descendants.

4. Mosaic laws were given to impart an understanding of this relationship.

5. Jerusalem and its temple were destroyed as the Israelites continued to sin against God.

6. The post-exilic prophets prophesied the coming of a more glorious new Jerusalem.

7. Jesus, as God's incarnate, came to restore this relationship.

8. Jesus's death and resurrection broke the power of sin, and paved the way of direct access to God's throne of grace.

9. Jesus promised that if we prayed in his name, our prayers will be answered to the glorification of the Father.

10. Prayer was not the ultimate, but the penultimate, pointing to the day that we will see God face to face as we are truly known.

11. Prayer is the royal road to God's throne of Grace.

CHARACTERISTICS OF EFFECTIVE PRAYER

The following are some of my personal reflections to Chester's theses.

THE LORD'S PRAYER: the quintessential example of an effective prayer

As God has invited us to enter into His throne of grace and partake in the privilege of fellowship with Him, how should we pray and converse with Him?

In the Gospel of Luke, Jesus' disciples asked him to teach them to pray, just as John the Baptist taught his disciples (Luke 11:1). Jesus taught them the Lord's Prayer.

>Our Father which art in heaven,
>Hallowed be thy name.
>Thy kingdom come.
>Thy will be done, as in heaven, so in earth.
>Give us this day our daily bread.
>And forgive us our sins; for we also forgive every one that is
>   indebted to us.
>And lead us not into temptation; but deliver us from evil."
>   (Luke 11:2-5, KJV; also, Matthew 6:9-13, NIV).

The first 4 lines were directed to God. The creator of heaven and earth has become our Father. What a privilege! Chester pointed out that the context of the Lord's Prayer was one of eschatological in expectation (159). Praying to our Father in heaven anticipates us to be included in the Trinitarian fellowship (159). His name is holy and we must be holy like Him. As his people, we deeply yearn for God to establish His kingdom on earth. The Lord's Prayer is a prayer for the consummation of the kingdom of God at the end of time that only God can bring (162).

The next three lines addressed our needs. They reminded us to be grateful for the divine provision of our daily manna, that God is sufficient to meet all our needs. As God has sent His son to pay for the debts of our sins at the cross, we should emulate Him to truly forgive those who have transgressed against us. God does not tempt us. In our daily testing and trials, we must let God work in us to choose good and not evil.

The line "for thine is the kingdom, and the power, and the glory, for ever, Amen" was an earlier addition incorporated in liturgical use, but was not recorded in the original gospel (158). Yet, it sums up the yearning of His people for the fulfillment of the kingdom, power, and glory of God.

Thus, the Lord's Prayer is a prayer for the future that also prompts us to walk with God in the present (166).

After giving the Lord's Prayer, Jesus illustrates the power of friendship in a parable.

A person went to his friend at midnight asking to lend him three loaves of bread. This person had a friend who came from a journey to him at night, and this person had nothing to set before him (Luke 11:5-6). Despite the inconvenient hour (the door was shut, his children asleep, and he cannot rise and give his friend what's needed), Jesus said that his friend will rise and give him as many loaves of bread as he needed [because he *is* his *friend*, and because of the opportunity friendship offers] (Luke 11:5-9). Then Jesus added:

> Ask, and it shall be given to you;
> Seek, and you shall find;
> Knock, and the door will be opened to you. (Luke 11:9-10, NIV)

The great lesson here is that God will answer prayer in Christ's name not only because we are God's children, but also we are His friends. The freedom, intimacy, and openness of asking and conversing between friends are ours to implore. And Jesus promised the ultimate gift, "If you then, though you are evil, know how to give good gifts to your children, how much more will your Father in heaven give the Holy Spirit to those who ask him" (Luke 11:13).

To have the Holy Spirit in the Triune God in us is the ultimate source of psychospiritual empowerment. "God in us and we in God", what more do we need to ask? Paul said, "If God is for us, who can be against us?" (Romans 8:31)

EFFECTIVE PRAYERS

The New Testament cautions us how not to pray:
- Do not pray like the hypocrites (Matthews 6:5).
  In Matthews 6, Jesus warned us not to pray like the hypocrites standing in the synagogues and on the street corners to be seen by men. Rather, we should do it in private. And in leading congregational prayer, we should remember that we pray not to impress people, but to bring our collective yearning, adoration, and petition to God.

- Do not babble like pagans (Mathews 6:7).
  To babble is to pray like pagans. God knows our needs before we ask Him. Be brief and straightforward in our asking. It's not the quantity of words that counts, as the spinning of a prayer wheel demands; rather, as Calvin says, "true prayer is an unburdening of the hearts." (156) Ecclesiastes reminds us, "God is in heaven and you are on earth, so let your words be few." (5:2)

Chester further amplified the rules for effective prayers in the New Testament.
1. Pray to the Father directly. When Jesus prayed, he addressed the first person of the triune God as Father. (39) The Lord's Prayer also begins with "our Father." It is

a privilege to come directly to the God's throne of grace, and pray directly to the Father.

2. Pray in Christ's name. Christ is the only mediator between God and man. (1 Timothy 2:5) He has paved the way for us to approach boldly into the throne of Grace. (Hebrews 4:16) He is the permanent High Priest who is able to save completely those who come to God through him because he always lives to intercede for them. (Hebrews 7:25) Thus, we pray in Jesus' name not only as we would customarily mention his name at the conclusion of a prayer, but also in all sincerity and acknowledgment of the sacrifices Christ has made as our High Priest.

3. Pray in the Spirit. As children of God, Jesus promised us the indwelling of the Holy Spirit (John 16:7). Through Christ, we have access to the Father by one Spirit (Ephesians 2:18). The Spirit "groans" in us for the final liberation from sin and death (Romans 8:26). The Spirit helps us pray. Jude tells his readers to pray in the Spirit (Jude 20). Words may fail us, but since God knows that the Spirit desires what God desires, the Spirit prays for us without words (69). Chester quoted C.S. Lewis, "Prayer in its most perfect state is a soliloquy…If the Holy Spirit speaks in the man, then in prayer God speaks to God" (69).

Hence, the New Testament addresses prayer to the Father through the Son by, or with the aid of, the Holy Spirit. (39)

4. Pray with faith. (James 1:6)

The author of the book of James had this to say:
If any of you lacks wisdom, he should ask God, who gives generously to all without finding faults, and it will be given to him. But when he asks, he must believe and not doubt, because he who doubts is like a wave of the sea, blown and tossed by the wind. That man should not think he

will receive anything from the Lord; he is a double-minded man, unstable in all he does. (James 1:5-8)

Here, wisdom means making connections: connections between trials and suffering, God's purpose and character, seeing cause and effects in an ordered universe (77). In dream, Solomon asked for wisdom, a discerning heart to govern God's people, and to distinguish between right and wrong (1 Kings 3:9). The Lord was pleased that Solomon had asked for wisdom, and He gave him more than what he had asked for (1 Kings 3:10-14).

5. Pray with the right motive. (James 4:3)

James further stated:
> ...You do not have, because you do not ask God. When you ask, you do not receive, because you ask with wrong motives, that you may spend what you get on your pleasures. (James 4:2-3)

6. [Pray with passion.] (Daniel 9:4-19)

Listen to Daniel in how he prayed.
> Now, our God, hear the prayers and petitions of your servant. For your sake, O Lord, look with favor on your desolate sanctuary. Give ear, O God, and hear; open your eyes and see the desolation of the city that bears your Name. We do not make requests of you because we are righteous, but because of your great mercy.. O Lord, listen! O Lord, forgive! O Lord, hear and act! For your sake, O my God, do not delay, because your city and your people bear your Name. (Daniel 17-19)

The Lord of heaven and earth responded by sending the angel Gabriel to tell Daniel, "As soon as you began to pray, an answer was given" (Daniel 9:23).

In New Testament theology, the author of the Book of James advocated for the inseparability between faith and action. Faith without action is dead (James 2:17). Thus, when James spoke about prayer, he made sure we understand the condition in which God answers them. It is for the furtherance of God's will, for the edification of others, and not for the fulfillment of one's pleasures. It must be anchored in an unshakable faith. And it must flow out of righteousness. James asserted, "The prayer of a righteous man is powerful and effective" (James 4:16).

Once flying over the Pacific Ocean, our plane met air turbulence. At first, passengers tried to sleep, read, or distract themselves with other activities. But then the plane shook more uncontrollably. The bouncing and careering of that huge hulk felt as if we were about to be unhinged from the sky. Worse, the turbulence lasted more than an hour, and we felt being tortured for eternity. At that moment, I began to hear a chanting at the back seat. A woman was praying out loud to calm herself. In an emergency situation, when no measures of help appeared forthcoming, we learn to look upward and to plead for help. But the power of prayer and meditation to reduce stress doesn't have to wait till urgent situation arises. You can learn to pray under any situation. St. Paul admonished us, "Be joyful always; pray continually; give thanks in all circumstances, for this is God's will for you in Christ Jesus" (1 Thessalonians 5:16).

Prayer draws God near to us.

Prayer is empowering because it is the royal road to God's throne of grace.

Chapter 17. KEY POINTS

1. Prayer is the conversation of friends.

2. God's grace invited us to join his Trinitarian fellowship through prayer.

3. Adam and Eve sinned, and sin broke this relationship with God.

4. God began a process of reconciliation through Abraham to have a people of His own.

5. Jesus's sacrificial love restored this relationship, and enabled us to become children and friends of God.

6. The indwelling of the Holy Spirit helps us pray. In this special friendship with God, God will grant us our petition.

7. Jesus promised that our prayer would be answered if we pray in His name.

8. Pray with faith, the right motives, conviction and passion. The prayer of a righteous man is powerful and effective.

9. Prayer is empowering because it is the royal road to God's throne of grace.

CHAPTER 18

The Power To Accept Suffering: Reframing The Meaning Of Pain And Illness

And after the fire came a gentle whisper (I King 19:12)

While in Babylon and Persia, Daniel's life and faith were constantly being tested. (Part 1) He also endured tremendous stress when he sought vision (Part 2). Yet, each time Daniel emerged from his trials spiritually stronger. What can you learn from him?

When you suffer a heart attack, cancer, depression; being maligned, misunderstood, harmed by others; face infidelity of trusted partner, or possibly facing death–you may ask, "Why does this illness or event happen to me? Why am I suffering? What is the meaning of my illness and suffering?" Is part of my body machine broken? Is it an attack from the devil, a lesson from God or a warning signal to change?

The story of Job in the Old Testament has long taught us that illness and healing have meanings. Studies of illness and healing practices across culture have amply documented the important role of symbolic healing and healing rituals, both in primitive and modern society. [47] Research has shown how you appraise stress may be a key mechanism for cellular aging.[48] Put simply, when you suffer, you may ask questions that probe the meaning of your illness. How you appraise your experience may influence the course of treatment you take and may determine whether you emerge from the illness stronger or weaker.

For example, two persons, both in their 40's, were suddenly stricken by a heart attack. One became depressed, the other fully recovered. What made the difference? If you blame yourself for lack of discipline that resulted in over-eating, lack of exercise, over-stressed at work, and started imaging that you are going to die, no one will care for your family, it's easy to get depressed. On the other hand, if you concentrate on the here-and-now, take advantage of the period of recovery to assess what may have contributed to your heart attack, develop a new strategy to maintain the functional integrity of your remaining heart muscle, and to change your lifestyle in order to achieve a better level of health, you can emerge from such an episode of illness a stronger, healthier, and happier individual. Thus, the way you respond to the symbolic meaning of illness may plunge you into despair and depression, or propel you to a speedier recovery and a higher level of health. Reframing the meaning of pain and illness is critical.

The power of symbolic healing and reframing the meaning of suffering has been well documented in a study on the emotional causes and resolution of emotional stress among a group of contemplative nuns.

In an article entitled, *Dark Night of the Soul*, Dura-Vila and colleagues conducted an ethnographic study of contemplative nuns in their attribution of their causes and resolution of emotional distress, with symptoms not unlike those of a clinical depression.[49] A psychiatrist/participant observer interviewed in Spanish ten contemplative

Augustinian nuns (8 permanent members, ages 49-76, average ~65 year and 2 novices, ages 21 and 27) over a period of three years. The semi-structured interviews were tape-recorded, verbatim transcribed, and content-analyzed. Relevant statements and the themes extracted from the data formed the key findings of the study.

Table 12 summarizes the emotional distress experienced by the nuns over time and their coping strategies. The importance of the *Dark Night of the Soul* as a model and metaphor of religiously motivated coping strategy was highlighted and elaborated.

Unlike other studies in which nuns belonged to active-life orders, this study focused on a group of contemplative nuns who were cloistered and leading a life devoted to prayer. Facing spiritual crises and experiencing symptoms not unlike those of a clinical depression, the sisters' religious choice and beliefs helped them carry on their lives with hope, trust and self-esteem.

Their sufferings, both emotional and physical, involved a connection to the divine. In contrast to psychiatric and medical view that tended to cast these symptoms as an illness, the nuns considered emotional distress as a chance for growth. Their distresses, described metaphorically as *Dark Night of the Soul,* imbued the suffering with meaning and transformed psychological distress into an active process for self-reflection and an opportunity for catharsis and spiritual growth.

The power of symbolic healing is even more apparent in psychotherapeutic cure. Jerome Frank, M.D., in his classic work on how psychotherapy works stated.

> All psychotherapeutic endeavors, whatever their form, transpire entirely in the realm of meanings. All psychotherapy depends on the fact that human thinking, feeling and behavior are guided largely by the person's assumption about reality, that is, meaning that he or she attributes to events or experiences, rather than their objective properties.[50]

From a psycho-spiritual perspective, illness and healing, as in Daniel's interpretation of Nebuchadnezzar's dream of the big tree (See chapter 4), connote spiritual and moral meaning. For non-believers, an illness episode may jolt one to evaluate one's value systems, direction in life, or simply ignoring its warning signals. For believers, the illness and healing experience usually carry "hidden lessons from God." It's up to you to discern them. Let me illustrate this from a recent illness and healing experience that I have had, and also from the testimony of the terminal experience of that of my pastor, the late Rev. Stephen Chiu.

THE WHISPER OF THE LORD AFTER THE FIRE

In November 2010, I was hospitalized for a week for hyponatremia (low serum sodium level). My serum sodium level had dropped from a normal of 135 mmol/liter to 108 mmol/liter. Had it dropped further, I may likely experience seizure, which could become life threatening.

The hyponatremic condition developed fairly rapidly over a week from complications with "flu", and possibly from long-term side effect of anti-hypertensive drug.

Over a few days, my flu symptoms worsened. First the hiccups, then a flare-up of my migraine headache, and finally, vomiting. When taken to the emergency room, I was weak, unsteady on my feet, couldn't concentrate and remember well. I could hardly lift a pen to sign admission paper. My signature was almost illegible. My serum sodium level had dropped from a normal of 135 mmol/liter to 108 mmol/liter. I was hospitalized for a week.

To a non-believer, my illness can be viewed simply as complications from flu. Nothing extraordinary. But to me, since I believe that illness has meanings, I had plenty of time to reflect, pray, and meditate on the lessons God may be teaching me, "What is the whisper of the Lord after the fire?" (I King 19:12) I learned the following lessons.

First, a deeper realization of the love and care from my wife, and knowing whom my true friends are. My wife, Tina, has always stood with me all through life's challenges. But during acute illness, her love shines even much brighter. Throughout this illness, I also came to realize who are my true friends, people the Chinese considered, "Who knows the echo of your hearts." It's important to further cultivate and enlarge such friendship particularly after retirement. In addition to my wife, these are people I could count on when the chips are down.

Second, reordering my priorities. Upon my retirement, I have been pursuing two tracks of activities: planning on research on psychosocial factors in sudden cardiac death; and Christian witnessing through talks, workshops, presentations, and writing. My research on Daniel was delayed and distracted by other activities. I decided to reorder my priorities, postponed all other tasks until I finish the book on Daniel. (See also chapter 14 on the events leading to this decision.)

I also learned to implement a more effective time- and stress-management strategy. I learned not to cramp too many tasks within a short period of time, even though they may all appeared to be worthwhile. When illness began to occur, I must give myself enough time to rest, allow time to recuperate, treat them aggressively, and not let things slide. I reviewed with my doctor to change a couple of my medications.

Third, rebuilding my body strength. As I'm convinced as St. Paul did, that our body is the temple of the Holy Spirit (I Corinthians 6:19), it is essential that I keep my body in as good a condition as possible for the glory of God. Thus, I must rebuild my strength and energy. After hospitalization, I decided to gradually add on bicycling, gym workouts, or swimming, in addition to my daily hourly walk.

PASTOR STEPHEN CHIU'S ILLNESS AND TESTIMONY

My late pastor, the Rev. Stephen Chiu, was a simple, sincere, learned, and dedicated man of God. He was stricken with lung cancer before he died. He suffered through severe bouts of dyspnea (difficulty of breathing). Many friends visited and prayed for him. Yet, when one visited him, a marvelous thing happened: one was left being comforted by him instead of the other way around. In a letter scribbled with weakened handwriting to his friends and congregant, and read after his death, he testified how his severe dyspnea made him realized deeply the suffering and suffocation of Christ on the Cross. Like the experience of the Augustinian nuns mentioned earlier, Pastor Chiu endured and transformed the meaning of his suffering into a final step of spiritual enlightenment and liberation. He used his suffering as an opportunity to help others. He triumphed over death.

In summary, many of us may suffer illness. Each illness episode has a spiritual lesson, a gentle whisper after fire. Each illness is a crisis, an opportunity to examine the "dangerous opportunity" as the word "crisis" means in Chinese. How you appraise stress may determine whether you tilt toward health or illness. If you focus on the danger, you'll likely become despaired, discouraged, and even depressed. But if you focus on the opportunities, you are apt to emerge from the episode of illness, even stronger and wiser. As Dr. Robert Schuller Sr. of the *Hour of Power* repeatedly admonished, "Turn your scars into stars." St. Paul mentioned, "And we know in all things God works for the good of those who love him, who have been called according to his purpose" (Romans 8:28). Yes, all things, including suffering and illness.

Table 12. Sources of stress and their coping strategies of ten Augustinian nuns in a Spanish monastery, 2006-2008

Sources of Stress	Coping strategy
"Profound spiritual suffering and desolation" (556)	"Considered this period of spiritual angst and suffering to be a natural stage of the spiritual development, intrinsically associated with a process of spiritual growth and maturation" (556)
"Suffering from low mood, dissatisfaction, uneasiness, lack of volition and interest, low self-esteem, tearfulness and frequent inability to concentrate and to pray" (556)	"Maintained their [daily] activities and only rarely missed prayers or manual duties" (556) "Trust in God and they never lost hope" (556)
Moments of temporary distress (557)	Viewed these as a reminder of " 'the many valuable lessons learnt thanks to it'… spiritual growth as the principal benefit of the Dark Night of the Soul…'decades of sadness' was a necessary process of maturation and purification of her soul, an in-depth learning experience and an intensive transformative experience of …religious life." (557)
"Dark Nights" (558)	"A chance… to imitate Christ in the suffering of his Passion… and to reinforce their condition of 'wives of Christ'… sure of always being accompanied by God" (558)
"Doubting choice of religious life" (559)	"To have clear goals and to remember their original commitment…to be life-long, drawing parallel between religious and marriage vows" (559)

"Foregoing marriage and childbearing" (560)	"…believe that not having an exclusive love for their own biological children enables them to be 'mothers of the whole humanity" (560)
"Relationship Problems" (561)	"Serving the community and putting the well-being of the community above the individual nun's needs or wishes" (561)
"Environmental stressors"(561)	"… providing meaning to the experience of a negative event, transforming and incorporating it into their life of prayer " (561)
"Fear of the contemplative Life Becoming Extinct [decrease in numbers entering vocation]" (561)	"Trusting that God will always take care of them, but also showing a practical and realistic approach (to merge several monasteries and admission of sisters from other countries]" (562)
"Suffering, Illness and death" (562)	Regarded "concept of Heaven as a reward for the suffering involved in death as well as for the coherence and goodness of their lives…death becomes a transition to a much better existence" (562) "They have the conviction that they were going to be looked after by their Sisters until death and not only looked after in a physical sense, but also being spiritually enveloped and sustained in their faith and hope of an eternal life" (563) "Reflecting on the Passion of Christ. The way he endured his sufferings 'with generosity, faith, strength and hope'." (563)

Source: *Adapted from* Dura-Vila, G., Dein, S., Littlewood, R., and Leavey, G. *The Dark Night of the Soul:* Causes and Resolution of emotional Distress Among Contemplative Nuns. *Transcultural Psychiatry* 2010 47:548.

Chapter 18: KEY POINTS

1. How you appraise stress may determine whether your experience of illness tilts toward health or illness.

2. During suffering and illness, seek and understand God's will, the "gentle whisper after fire."

3. Focus on the positive meanings of your experience to emerge from illness episodes stronger and wiser.

4. Psychospirituality can empower you by reframing the meaning of illness, and focusing on the positives.

CHAPTER 19

The Power Of Resilience And Hope: Bouncing Back From Adversities

> For everything that was written in the past was
> written to teach us, so that through endurance and the
> encouragement of the Scriptures we might have hope
> (Romans 15:4)

D aniel's life was a beacon of hope for his people. He always bounced back from stress and suffering. His longevity lasted from King Nebuchadnezzar's period through the early Persian King Darius's reign. Besides his spiritual quality, what personality factors might have contributed to his longevity and made him such a shining and resilient star? And how can you also acquire resilient traits?

When CNN flashed the news about the death of Elizabeth Edwards, wife of the former Democratic presidential candidate, John Edwards, the story of her life touched many hearts. Elizabeth battled through the early tragic death of her son, Wade, in a car accident; breast cancer; and her husband's indiscretion near the end of her life. She captured her experiences in a book entitled *Resilience*. (Edwards, Elizabeth, 2009) [51]

What is resilience? The image of a stretched rubber band bouncing back to form comes to mind. Resilience connotes such a meaning. If your life is stressed to the limit, can you bounce back? What makes a person cope effectively under stress while another breaks down? What are the qualities that make successful coping?

Daniel went through a lot of challenges in his life. The stresses he faced could have easily sent many to early retirement, mental and physical breakdown, or confinement to an asylum. He bounced back each time from the crisis and became spiritually stronger. That is resilience. What were his secrets? Three traits were apparent:

First, Daniel had a strong, healthy body. Daniel didn't indulge in eating food that would harm his body and undermine his faith. Not that all the king's foods and drinks were bad. But he avoided foods considered morally contaminated according to his Jewish custom. He and his friends thrived on a vegetarian diet. To be resilient, you have to protect your body from harm, and guard your soul. Nowadays, with rampant environmental pollutants everywhere, it's hard to avoid them. You can hardly walk the streets without inhaling second-hand, cancer-causing cigarette smoke. The food you eat sometimes may contain unhealthy chemicals or fertilizers. There are just too much junk food and drinks to tempt you, to skip exercise. All kinds of worldly ideologies compete for your attention, and want to win over your allegiance. How do you prevail? Psychospirituality reminds you that your body is the temple of God. You have to respect and keep it clean so that you can become a better and more effective instrument to be used by God.

Second: Daniel possessed strong character traits that exuded confidence, loyalty, humility, dedication, care, altruism and love. Daniel was so grounded and personable that whoever came in contact with him, admired and loved him. He was able to cultivate the friendship of his captors, Arioch, and the guards. He gained the trust of all the Babylonian and Persian kings. His character and work ethics were so impeccable--without even a hint of corruption or negligence in duty--that the only way his enemies could find any ground for charges against him had to be something to do with his faith (Daniel 6:5).

Third, Daniel had an abiding faith and trust in God. At the innermost core of his being, Daniel and his three friends maintained a steadfast connection with their Almighty God. This relationship was of such psychospiritual strength that even when they were facing the threat of death, they were unafraid. They would rather die than succumb to worshipping idol. Listen to the ringing faith of his three friends before they were thrown into the fiery furnace.

> "But even if he [God] does not [save us from death], we want you to know, O king, that we will not serve your gods or worship the image of gold you have set up." (Daniel 3:18)

Relying on psychospirituality can enhance your motivation to promote physical fitness; cultivate a winning, authentic, and pleasing personality; acquire correct work ethics; diligence; and a strong faith. These are skills associated with resilience that can inoculate you against stress and illness. The good news about resilience is that these traits and quality can be learned and adopted.

Dennis Charney, M.D., Ph.D., dean of research and a professor of psychiatry at Mt. Sinai School of Medicine, and Steven Southwick, M.D., a professor of psychiatry at Yale University, identified personality traits associated with resilience in a study of 250 America POWs during the Vietnam War. These prisoners were held up for up to eight years, subjected to torture and solitary confinement but showed a remarkable lower-than-expected incidence of depression and PTSD years after their release. [52] When their traits were compared to the characteristics of a group of women who had suffered severe trauma, especially physical and sexual abuse, and a group who showed courage and resilience while facing serious medical problems, they found that the same characteristics of resilience in the POWs were present in these other two studies as well. These 10 characteristics consisted of developing optimism, cognitive flexibility, a personal moral compass or shatterproof set of beliefs, altruism, finding a resilient role model in a member or a heroic figure, learning to be adept at facing fears, developing active coping skills and seeking support from others, establishing and nurturing a supportive network, exercise, and having a sense of humor and laugh frequently.

Almost all of the above traits could be found in Daniel's personality and experience. A man of faith doesn't remain passive, but actively seeks ways to cope with stress, and drawing resources from one's personality, relationships, and spiritual reservoir.

Elizabeth Edward had to learn to accept, to let go, to refocus, and to rebuild her life after each of her storms. She wanted her grandchildren to be able to say that she stood in the storm, "When the wind did not blow her way–and it surely has not–she adjusted her sails." That is resilience.

The amygdala in the human brain acts like an emotional sentinel. It tells you where danger lies, generates certain normal amount of anxiety to prepare you to "flight" or "fight". Too much of the anxiety response can cause anxiety disorders and PTSD. But learning to modulate amygdala's responses to stress can be a strategy to develop resilience. Training using Cognitive Behavioral Technique (CBT) can be a useful way to learn resilience. Charney recommends training that engage emotions, intellect, morals and physical endurance–experiences Daniel had had. The story of Daniel also encourages us to also seek spiritual resources to buttress our resilience against all odds.

Chapter 19. KEY POINTS

1. Resilience and hope allow you to bounce back from adversities.

2. Daniel's resilience appears to be related to:

    a. A strong and healthy body;

    b. A personality that exudes confidence, loyalty, humility, dedication, care, altruism and love;

    c. An abiding faith and trust in God.

3. Elizabeth Edwards demonstrated how resilience helped her bounced back from adversities.

4. Psychospirituality can motivate you to cultivate ten ways to promote resilience.

CHAPTER 20

The Power Of Love:
Transcending And Transforming Acts

Love…always protects, always trusts,
always hopes, always perseveres
(1 Corinthians 13:7)

M any words can be used to describe Daniel, but one seemed to capture the essence of his character and spirituality – love -- love of God and his fellowmen. Daniel exuded that quiet, confident, edifying, timely, and uplifting love that "always protects, always trusts, always hopes, always perseveres", attributes that St. Paul had beautifully expounded in 1 Corinthians 13. Let's examine Daniel's love.

Daniel always protects. When his life, and that of his friends, and those of Babylonian wise men were on the line because of the inability of the Babylonian wise men to unravel Nebuchadnezzar's dream, young Daniel acted to protect. Arioch, commander of the king's guard, was set to carry out the king's execution order. When Daniel learned from Arioch the king's fury, he went to the king and asked for time so that he might interpret the dream for him. In effect, he delayed the execution order. In so doing, he put his life on the line. Remember, the young man had not yet been tested as a dream diviner. He was relying on pure faith that the Lord will reveal the king's dream to him. So, Daniel and his friends fervently prayed. And during the night, the mystery was revealed to Daniel in a vision.

Daniel always trusts. When Daniel learned that Persian King Darius had decreed that in the next thirty days, no one was to pray to any god but him, Daniel had a choice–to pray to his God, or defy the king's order (See chapter 6). He chose to continue praying to his God three times a day, as was his routine. No evil scheme from his enemies was going to deter or undermine his faith. When Daniel was thrown into the lions' den, it was the king who displayed more anxiety than Daniel did. The king, who realized that he had been tricked to issue the decree, said to Daniel, "May your God, whom you serve continually, rescue you" (Daniel 6:16). That night, the king returned to his palace without eating, and couldn't sleep. At the first light of dawn, the king got up and hurried to the lions' den to check out Daniel's fate and called him. Daniel answered, "My God sent his angel and he shut the mouth of the lions. They have not hurt me, because I was found innocent in his sight. Nor have I ever done any wrong before you, O king" (Daniel 6:21).

In chapter 9, when Daniel prayed and petitioned the Lord for the return of his people to rebuild Jerusalem, his prayer was expressed in a tone of absolute certainty that God would grant him his request. In fact, Gabriel, the angel sent by the Lord, said to him, "As soon as you began to pray, an answer was given" (Daniel 9:23).

Such was the trusting relation Daniel had with his God. He had a faith that also uplifted his people that shone brightly during the dark night of Israel's history.

Daniel always hopes. What can we say about the sentiment of this young Jewish youth and his friends, when, early in their lives, along with their defeated king, the king's royal cohort, and articles from the temple of God, they were exiled to King Nebuchadnezzar's Babylon?

Daniel and his friends had to endure the shame of a defeated people. They faced crisis after crisis that tested their faith. Just to survive, they were challenged to exercise the best of their knowledge, wisdom, tact, and diplomacy in a gentile court filled with intrigues, and under the constant jealous eyes of their enemies. Daniel must be wondering how long he would have to wait to rebuild Jerusalem and redeem the honor of his people and Jehovah's name. No wonder when he learned seventy years had lapsed as Jeremiah had predicted for the return of the exile to Judah, Daniel "turned to the Lord and pleaded with him in prayer and petition, in fasting, and in sackcloth and ashes" (Daniel 9:3). His prayer of contrition for his people, and to God to "turn away your anger and your wrath from Jerusalem, your city, your holy hills" (Daniel 9:16), and ending with a wrenching plea to Jehovah to forgive the sins of his people, testified to Daniel's singularly confident hope and love. He had waited all these times for this redeeming moment to arrive and he wasn't going to allow this opportunity to pass him by. No greater tribute can be paid to Daniel than that given to him by the angel at the end of his book, "As for you, go your way till the end. You will rest, and then at the end of the days you will rise to receive you allotted inheritance" (Daniel 12:13). That was the promise of resurrection. That was hope.

Daniel always perseveres. Through the danger of trials and seemingly hopeless situations, Daniel persevered. He persevered when his identity and name was changed to Belteshazzar, a reminder that he was now beholden to a foreign king and his god. He persevered when his skill at divining dream was tested to the limit. He persevered when his friends were thrown into the fiery furnace, for refusal to worship an idol, and that he could be the enemies' next target. When his king's mind had turned into that of an animal, he persevered by continuing to serve in the king's court, and waited out for his king to repent and recover. He persevered till the moment so that he could be summoned before Belshazzar to interpret the writings on the wall. He preserved when he waited for seventy years to end, as Jeremiah had prophesied, so that he could petition God to rebuild Jerusalem. He persevered through the epic changes of dynasties from Babylonia to Persia, to be summoned back to serve. Though he realized the emotional toil visionary experiences exacted on him, he persevered in seeking out the visions from the Lord to understand what the future had in store for Israel in the gentile world. With the burden of utmost personal emotional strain, he persevered to seek God' revelation to gaze into the future, and saw the coming of the Messiah, events at end time, and the establishment of the magnificent, glorious, and eternal kingdom of God. Yes, Daniel learned to be patient, to wait, to pray, to act, and to persevere. He knew his God never failed him.

THE POWER OF LOVE

What can you learn from Daniel's love? With all the ethnic, political and religious strives that seemed to tear our world apart, can love transcend racial, ethnic, political and religious difference, anger, hate, and violence as Daniel exemplified? Can you really love as St. Paul expounded in 1 Corinthians 13? Can you reach the highest plateau of love that St. Peter urged you to do, "from brotherly kindness to love for all people?" (2 Peter 1:7). Consider this true story reported by Wilson Scott about the power of love: *Life and Hope Flow From Palestinian Boy's Death*, that appeared in World News, The Washington Post, Saturday, November 12, 2005.

Ahmed Khatib was a 12-year-old Palestinian boy, who was mistakenly shot twice by Israeli soldiers on Nov. 3, 2005 at Jenin, West Bank, during the heat of street fighting near his house. The boy had been holding a toy gun. He died two days later in an Israeli hospital.

His parents made the surprising peace gesture by allowing his organs to be harvested for transplant to six people including five Israeli Jews were the recipient of the boy's heart, lungs, liver and kidneys. The family's gesture of love peace momentarily transformed the persistent Jewish/Palestinian conflict into a shared moment of love between two people.

The story of Khatib can inspire you to acquire this transforming love. Khatib's family had all the reasons to hate the Israeli for accidentally killing their boy. Yet, they turned their potential hatred into a supreme act of love by donating the boy's organs to save lives, even the lives of their perceived enemy. This is the kind of love that religion, and specifically Christianity, can and should impart and inspire--not through threat, not killing, nor acts of force or terror, but through act of transcending and transforming love. Christ epitomizes this love when he lived, died, and resurrected to show you the path to obtain this transforming power of love.

Daniel's psychospirituality actualized power of love. As with Christ, Daniel bids you to follow his example.

> Once you have flown,
> You will walk the Earth
> with your eyes turned skyward;
> for there you have been,
> there you long to return.
>
> --- Leonardo da Vince

Chapter 20: KEY POINTS

1. Daniel's love exemplified St. Paul's definition of love in 1Corinthians 13: "love…always protects, always trusts, always hopes, always perseveres."

2. The family of Ahmed Khatib exhibited the power of love that transcended and transformed hatred and political differences.

3. Psychospirituality can empower you to achieve love to transcend ethnic, religious, and political sentiment.

4. Both Daniel and Christ showed how to acquire this transforming love through faith in God.

5. Christ's sacrificial love can pave the way for you to obtain this power of love through faith in him.

CHAPTER 21

The Power To Live Longer: Resetting Lifestyle For Cellular Longevity

Some form of meditation may have salutary effects on telomere length by reducing cognitive stress and stress arousal and increasing positive states of mind and hormonal factors that may promote telomere maintenance (Elissa S. Epel, PhD)

INTRODUCTION

D aniel lived long. God's willing, so can you. While your life is in God's hand, and you do not know what will happen tomorrow (James 4:14), you can, like Daniel, use psychospirituality to engage in a lifestyle that increases the odds of adding years to your life.

Daniel was estimated to have lived more than 90 years. (See table 1) It may just be a coincidence that the alignment of Daniel's genetic endowment, environment, diet, lifestyle, and psychospirituality contributed to his longevity. But the fact that God blessed him and used his long career to accomplish His will, testified to how God can use you if you are willing. You, too, can use psychospirituality to cultivate a healthy, comprehensive life style that can add years to your life. And medical science is beginning to provide the data to support this assertion.

Recent medical discoveries, advances in medical research, availability of technological tools like brain imaging technique (functional MRI), powerful statistical analytic methods, and sophisticated research design have enabled researchers to engage in areas of study heretofore generally untouched by medical scientists. Such an area is psychospirituality. We now are at the threshold of better understanding the gene-spiritual connection. While data have yet to definitively elucidate gene-spiritual mechanism(s), research on psychological variables such as optimism, pessimism, "purpose in life", "locus of control", meditation, prayers, etc., and their effect on genes suggest that these variables, though not specifically classified under the psycho-spiritual label, appeared to overlap psychospiritual domain. Researches along this line could potentially illuminate the gene-spiritual connection. Religions have long traditions of prayer and meditation. Spirituality addresses meaning and purpose of life.[53] Data are accumulating that show psychospiritual practices such as prayer and mindfulness meditation can reduce cell-damaging psychological stress.[54,55] Compared to baseline, brain scan of cerebral blood flow of three Franciscan nuns during meditative prayer showed increased blood flow in the prefrontal cortex, inferior parietal lobes and inferior frontal lobes, areas of brain that are implicated in spiritual activity.[56] Psychospiritual attributes like having a "purpose in life" and enhancement of "locus of control" through reduction of negative personality traits, as well as modification of psychospiritual attitudes could enhance optimism and reduce pessimism. All these factors could potentially reduce stress, influence your gene and cellular activity, and by implication, your longevity.

In the pages that followed, you will be acquainted with the story of telomere and telomerase, and their relevance to psychospirituality and cellular longevity.

DISCOVERY OF TELOMERE AND TELOMERASE

In 2009, Elizabeth Blackburn, Carol W. Greider and Jack W. Szostak won the 2009 Nobel Prize in Medicine and Physiology for the discovery of how chromosomes are protected by telomeres and the enzyme telomerase.[57] What are telomere and telomerase?

TELOMERE AND TELOMERASE

Telomeres are DNA-protein complexes that cap chromosomal ends and promote chromosomal stability. Thus, telomere length can serve as a marker of biological age.[57]

Telomerase is an enzyme that repairs chromosomal ends and forestalls telomere shortening.[57] The stress hormone cortisol inhibits telomerase activity.[58]

In normal aging, the average, healthy adults lose about 30-60 base telomere pairs/year. But this is not invariable; some people actually lengthen telomeres.[59]

Significance of telomere and telomerase

The discovery of telomere and telomerase provided the scientific community a tool to measure the gene life and the factors that influence cellular longevity. By correlating the length of telomere and measuring the degree of telomerase enzymatic activity, scientists are now beginning to predict cell aging and longevity. Longer telomere means longer cellular life; shortened telomere, shorter cellular life. The following are some preliminary findings of shortened telomere length, and their implications for disease states.

Shortened telomere length and disease states

Studies have shown that individuals with shorter telomeres had poorer survival (OR= 3.18, heart disease).[60] Compared to non-stressed women, high stressed women showed signs of cellular aging, about 13 years older.[59] Furthermore, telomere shortening is associated with many disease states:

1.   Major Depression.[61]

2.   High phobic anxiety in women.[62]

3.   Cardiovascular disease and mortality in men.[63]

4.   Depression with coronary heart disease.[64]

5.   Vascular dementia.[65]

6.   Abdominal Obesity.[66]

7.   Insulin resistance.[67]

In addition, many behavioral factors are associated with telomere shortening, including:

1.   Chronic stress.[59]

2.   Pessimism.[68]

3.   Dietary Restraint.[69]

4.   Intimate partner violence.[70]

5.   Childhood trauma in PTSD.[71]

6.   Stress exposure in intrauterine life.[72]

7.   Midlife women with poor sleep quality.[73]

8.   Worse physical fitness in patients with coronary heart disease.[74]

9.   Acute stress.[75]

Epel and others have advanced possible biological mechanisms on how stress shortens telomere and dampens telomerase activity.

1. Hormonal. Stress acts through the hypothalamic/pituitary and adrenal gland axis that produces cortisol, the stress hormone.[76] Increase cortisol in chronic stress condition reduces telomerase activity and shortens telomere length.

2. Chronic inflammation. Inflammation causes elevation of certain bodily inflammatory enzymes like Interleukin-6 (IL-6). Cumulative Inflammatory Load (high levels of IL-6 and TNF-alpha [tumor necrosis factor-alpha], but not C-Reactive Protein, CRP) has been found to affect telomerase activity.[77] Mental attitude of pessimism, for example, correlates with leukocyte telomere shortness and elevated interleukin-6 in post-menopausal women.[68]

3. Oxidative stress. Chronicity in Major Depression, inflammation and oxidative stress are correlated with shortened telomere length.[78]

So far, studies have shown:
- Telomere length marks biological age in mitotic cells;
- Telomere length may be shortened in chronic stress and depression; this may result from cortisol, oxidative stress and chronic inflammation;
- Shortened telomere length is associated with many medical illnesses;
- Many behavioral factors–stress, pessimism, etc.–are correlated with shortened telomere.

THE GOOD NEWS

While telomere may be shortened, studies have also shown factors associated with telomere lengthening:
- Moderate physical activity.[79,80]
- Intake of Omega-3 Fatty Acid in patients with coronary heart disease.[81]

- Greater endogenous estrogen exposure in postmenopausal women at risk for cognitive decline.[82]
- Diabetes prevention in obese people with impaired glucose metabolism.[83]
- Comprehensive lifestyle changes.[84]
- Meditation (implied).[85]
- Reduction of stress.[86]

Comprehensive Lifestyle Changes

In 2008, Dean Ornish and associates provided preliminary data to indicate that comprehensive lifestyle changes, including meditation practice, are significantly associated with increase in telomerase activity and consequent telomere maintenance capacity in human immune-system cells.[84] Ornish et al.'s study asked 30 men with biopsy-diagnosed low-risk prostatic cancer to make comprehensive lifestyle change. Baseline telomerase activity was compared with post-treatment values after 3 months. The treatment protocol consisted of the following program:

- Diet: (low fat [10% calories from fat], whole food, plant-based high in fruits, vegetables, unrefined grain, legumes and low in carbohydrate; plus
- Diet supplements: soy (one daily serving tofu plus 58 g of a fortified soy protein powered beverage), Vit E. (100 IU daily), selenium (200 ug daily), and Vit C (2 gm. daily);
- Exercise: moderate aerobic (walking 30 minutes/day, 6 days/week);
- Stress management (gentle yoga-based stretching, breathing, meditation, imagery, and progressive relaxation techniques 60 minutes/day, 6 days/week), and a 1-hr group support session/week.

The Results revealed:

- Plasma Blood Mononuclear Cell (PBMC) telomerase activity expressed as natural logarithms increased from 2.00 (SD 0.44) to 2.22 (SD 0.49; p+0.031).
- Raw values increased from 8.05 (SD 3.50) units to 10.38 (SD 6.01) standard arbitrary unit.
- The increases in telomerase activity were significantly associated with decreases in low-density lipoprotein (LDL) cholesterol and decreases in psychological stress.

The authors concluded that comprehensive lifestyle changes are significantly associated with increase in telomerase activity and consequent telomere maintenance capacity in human immune-system cells.

While the sample size is small, such findings, if duplicated with a larger group and with control, and the teasing out specific factor of diet, exercise, and stress management technique, including meditation, could clarify the specific factor of health-enhancing effect of applying comprehensive life style changes to lengthen cellular life. Psychospiritual practices may be implicated to enhance this change.

PSYCHOSPIRITUALITY, TELOMERE AND TELOMERASE

Can psychospirituality reflected in practices such as prayer, mindfulness meditation, reduction of pessimism as well as changes in spiritual values (purpose in life) and "locus of control" and comprehensive life style slow rate of cellular aging?

In a review article, D. Williams & M.J. Sternthal (2007) have shown that higher level of religious attendance is predictive of a strong and consistent and often graded reduction in mortality rate.[87] Exactly what may be the mechanism is unclear. The authors speculated that health practices and social ties are important pathways by which religion can affect health. Other potential pathways include the provision of systems of meaning and feeling of strength to cope with stress and adversity.[87]

More recently, correlational studies between mindfulness-based stress reduction (MBSR) and telomere length and telomerase activity have shown that certain personality traits like optimism and pessimism, purpose in life and "locus of control" affect telomerase activity and telomere length. Here are some of the concepts and research findings:

MINDFULNESS MEDITATION

Mindfulness meditation involves the development of awareness of present-moment experience with a compassionate, non-judgmental stance. Through attentional training you may enhance control of your thoughts and feelings, thereby allowing redirection of attention away from ruminative thinking and back to the present. [88,89]

Mindfulness-based stress reduction (MBSR) technique is now accepted into the mainstream of psychiatric and psychological healing practices. Even within an academically health environment, introduction of MBSR was well received. MBSR effectively reduced self-reported stress with effects lasting for at least 1 year and increased the daily spiritual experiences of participants. [90]

PURPOSE IN LIFE

Purpose in life is defined as a sense of overarching meaning (extending beyond a particular situation) affects health outcomes via changes in specific psychological mediators (e.g. changes in appraisal or coping mechanisms that reduce negative affect).[91] As a psychological variable, it has been shown that the amount of weekly time spent in "loving-kindness" meditation predicted a cumulative, daily increase in positive emotion over a 2-month period. This increase contributed to an increase in life satisfaction and reduced depressive symptoms via mediation of purpose of life and mindfulness.[92]

Furthermore, maintenance of a positive outlook during acute stress protects against pro-inflammatory reactivity and future depressive symptoms.[93]

LOCUS OF CONTROL

Your sense of internal locus of control influences responses to stressful events by improving coping strategies.[94]

High trait neuroticism or trait negative affectivity such as chronically and characteristically feeling tense, anxious, moody, or insecure amplifies stress responses in humans.[95]

In a study, effects of a 3-month meditation retreat on telomerase activity and two major contributors to the experience of stress, Perceived Control (associated with decreased stress) and Neuroticism (associated with increased subjective distress) revealed post-retreat telomerase activity was significantly greater in the retreat group ($p < 0.05$, Error bars: ±1SEM).[85]

- Increases in Perceived Control (associated with decrease stress) and decreases in Negative Affectivity (associated with increased subjective distress) contributed to increase in telomerase activity.
- Meditative practice influences Purpose in Life and directly affects both perceived control and negative emotionality, directly and indirectly affecting telomerase activity.

PESSIMISM AND OPTIMISM

Pessimism implies "less expectation for the future" -- the mental attitude of thinking the "cup is always half empty."

Optimism, on the other hand, implies "more expectation for the future" -- the mental attitude of thinking the "cup is always half full."

Studies have shown that the combination of less positive and more negative expectations for the future (i.e., lower optimism and higher pessimism) increases risk for disease and early mortality. O'Donovan et al. investigated whether dispositional tendencies towards optimism and pessimism were associated with telomere length (TL) and interleukin-L (IL-6) in a sample of 36 healthy post-menopausal women. Their results revealed pessimism was independently associated with shorter TL (β = –.68, p =.001) and higher IL-6 concentrations (β =.50, p =.02). In contrast, optimism was not independently associated with either measure TL and IL-6. These findings suggest dispositional pessimism may increase IL-6 and accelerate rate of telomere shortening.[68]

MINDFULNESS MEDITATION AND ITS EFFECTS ON BRAIN'S GRAY MATTER

Holzel and colleagues at the Massachusetts General Hospital recently reported a study that shows mindfulness practice leads to increases in regional brain gray matter density.[96] In an 8-weeks Mindfulness-Based Stress Reduction Program (MBSR), pre-post changes in brain gray matter concentration of 16 healthy participants who had never received meditation were compared with a waiting list control group of 17 subjects. The results showed increases in left hippocampus, posterior cingulate cortex, temporo-parietal junction, and cerebellum density in MBSR group compared to control. These brain regions are involved in learning and memory processes, emotion regulation, self-referential processing, and perspective taking.

Holzel et al.'s study powerfully shows that psychospiritual thoughts can actually sculpt the architectural domain of your brain.

The upshot of current mindfulness and telomere research findings seemed to suggest the following:

1. Psychological stress cognitions, particularly appraisals of threat and ruminative thoughts, can lead to prolonged state of reactivity. [48]

2.   Mindfulness meditation techniques appear to shift cognitive appraisals from threat to challenge, decrease ruminative thought, and reduce stress arousal. Mindfulness may also directly increase positive arousal state. [86]

3.   Some form of meditation may have salutary effects on telomere length by reducing cognitive stress and stress arousal and increasing positive states of mind and hormonal factors that may promote telomere maintenance.[86]

4.   Mindfulness-Based Stress Reduction (MBSR) increases regions of brain's gray matter.[96]

CONCLUSION

Review of preliminary data suggests that psychological variables of meditative prayers, mindfulness, "purpose in life", "locus of control", pessimism and optimism, and motivation towards healthy comprehensive life style changes, may influence telomere and telomerase activities. These psychological variables appeared to overlap with psychospiritual domain and potentially can open the door to a better understanding of a gene-spiritual connection. Promoting positive psychospiritual values and practices that reduce stress, chronic inflammatory processes, and oxidative injury to cells through enhancement of "purpose of life", increased sense of internal "locus of control", mindfulness, reduction of pessimism, and promotion of better compliance with healthy comprehensive lifestyle changes could affect gene's longevity. By reducing factors that shorten telomeres and increasing those that lengthen them, psychospiritual practices may potentially increase cellular life and immune cell longevity, and empower you to live longer.

Chapter 21: KEY POINTS

1. Telomeres are DNA-protein complexes that cap chromosomal ends and promote chromosomal stability. They serve as a marker of biological age.

2. Telomerase is an enzyme that repairs chromosomal ends and forestalls telomere shortening. The stress hormone cortisol inhibits telomerase activity.

3. Chronic Stress shortens telomere length.

4. Mindfulness reduces stress and increase brain's gray matter.

5. Promotion of psychospiritual values and practices such as optimism (reduction of pessimism), "purpose in life", and "locus of control" could increase telomere length.

6. Cultivating psychospiritual values and activities and promotion of a healthy comprehensive life style changes could lengthen you cellular life.

CHAPTER 22

The Power Of Prophecy: Emotional Preparedness For End Time

Therefore keep watch, because you do not know the
day or the time [of Christ's second coming]
(Matthew 25:13)

An outstanding feature of the book of Daniel is prophecy, specifically, predictions about end-time events. Yet, writing and predicting future events are controversial. But contemporary men do try to anticipate futures all the time. You want to know, plan, and be prepared on what's coming. You have weather reports, economic indicators, and instruments to predict earthquake, tsunami, tornados, and other natural disasters. Doctors make diagnosis on diseases based on symptoms, signs, and laboratory tests, and try to prognosticate the future course of disease. So, in the same spirit, we shall examine Daniel's apocalyptic visions.

Eschatology is the theological term employed to designate the doctrine of the last things, particularly those dealing with the second coming of Christ, and the events preceding or following this great event. [97] Eschatology has been and should be an important subject of biblical and psychological study. However, many people, including evangelical Christians and even some seminary professors, are reluctant to touch this subject. Unfortunately, some over-zealous evangelical preachers have undermined an objective examination of biblical eschatology, and made a mockery of it by predicting a definite time for the end of the world, only to see events passed by without any incidence. The Bible indicates that nobody, even Christ himself, knows the exact end time. Only God the Father knows (Matthew 24:36). But the book of Daniel clearly laid out signs of prophetic events. Daniel's prophecy about end-time events was mentioned in chapters 2, 7, 9, 10, 11, and 12. These prophecies were conveyed through symbols in dream and vision. Consider the following passages:

- Nebuchadnezzar dreamed of the large stature (chapter 2), and the appearance a rock cut out of a mountain, but not by human hands, that struck the stature and broke the iron, the bronze, the clay, the silver, and the gold to pieces. The rock became a huge mountain and filled the whole earth (Daniel 2:34-35). Daniel interpreted this vision as "the God of heaven will set up a kingdom that will never be destroyed, nor will it be left to another people. It will crush all those kingdoms and bring them to an end, but it will itself endure forever (Daniel 2:44).

- In Daniel's dream of the four beasts (chapter 7), the vision of the splendid "Ancient of Days" appeared, taking His seat on the throne. As the court was seated, and the books were opened, Daniel saw "the beast was slain and its body destroyed and thrown into the blazing fire. (The other beasts had been stripped of their authority, but were allowed to live for a period of time)" (Daniel 7:9-12).

Then before him was "one like a son of man, coming with the clouds of heaven. He approached the Ancient of Days and was led into his presence. He was given authority, glory and sovereign power; all peoples, nations, and men of every language worshipped him. His dominion is an everlasting dominion that will not pass away, and his kingdom is one that will never be destroyed" (Daniel 7:13).

• In the vision of the seventy "7s" (chapter 9), the angel Gabriel told Daniel, "After the sixty two 'sevens,' the Anointed one will be cut off and will have nothing. The people of the ruler who will come will destroy the city and sanctuary. The end will come like a flood: War will continue until the end, and desolations have been decreed. He, [the antichrist], will confirm a covenant with many for one 'seven.' In the middle of the 'seven' he will put an end to sacrifice and offering. And on a wing of the temple he will set up an abomination that causes desolation, until the end that is decreed is poured out on him" (Daniel 9:26-27).

• In Daniel's vision of the battle between the kings of the South and the North (chapter 11), a king will appear who will "exalt and magnify himself above every god and will say unheard of things against the God of gods. He will be successful until the time of wrath is completed, for what has been determined must take place" (Daniel 11:36).

• Daniel's vision in chapter 11 continues: "At that time Michael, the great prince who protects your people, will arise. There will be a time of distress such as has not happened from the beginning of nations until then. But at that time your people–everyone whose name is found written in the book–will be delivered. Multitudes who sleep in the dust of the earth will awake: some to everlasting life, others to shame and everlasting contempt" (Daniel 12:1-2).

These passages clearly predicted an end time; described end-time events, including the struggles between the ungodly and godly people; the termination of the human history; God's judgment; and the inauguration of God's eternal kingdom.

Jesus quoted Daniel's statement of "the abomination that causes desolation" when he discussed the signs of the end of the world (Matthew 24:15). Whereas Daniel's prophecies were in highly symbolic terms, Jesus's description was more elaborative and specific. Because of the confluence of Jesus and Daniel's discussion of the signs of the end time, it is appropriate at this point, to examine Jesus's discussion of the signs of the end time.

JESUS'S DESCRIPTION OF SIGNS OF THE END OF TIME

In Matthew 24-25, Jesus had a dialogue with his disciples about signs of the end time.

As Jesus and his disciples were walking away from the Jerusalem temple one day, the disciples called his attention to its building. Jesus then asked, "Do you see all these things?...I tell you the truth, not one stone here will be left on another; every one will be thrown down" (Matthews 24:2). Unsure of what this meant, later, at the Mount of Olives, the disciples came to Jesus privately and asked him, "Tell us, when will this happen, and what will be the sign of your coming and of the end of the age?" Jesus described the signs and also gave three parables to lead them into understanding the signs of the end time, and how to be emotionally prepared.

Question 1. "When will this [Christ's second coming and end time] happen?" (Matthew 24:3) – Jesus answered, "No one knows about that day or hour, not even the angels in heaven, nor the son, but only the Father" (Matthew 24:36). In spite of this indeterminate timing, Jesus urged the disciples to pay attention to the signs, "Now learn the lesson from the fig tree: As soon as its twigs get tender and its leaves come out, you can know that summer is near. Even so, when you see all these things, you know that it is near, right at the door" (Matthews 24:32-33).

Question 2. "What will be the sign of your coming and of the end of ages?"

Christ gave several signs:

1. Sign of falsehood, tribulations and catastrophe. The coming of deceivers who claimed to be Christ; hearing wars and rumors of wars; nations rising against nations, kingdom against kingdom; famines and earthquakes in various places; seeing standing in the holy place, and the fulfillment of the "the abomination that causes desolation" spoken of through the prophet Daniel (Matthews 24:5-7). Jesus used the metaphor of labor pains to describe the timing of these traumatic events. Like false labor pains preceding true ones, some of the signs may seem to be the beginning of the tribulations but are not yet indicative of the end of ages.

2. Sign of persecution of the believer, their falling away from faith, and the appearance of false prophets. Christ stated that because of him the believers will be handed over to be persecuted, put to death, and hated by all nations. Many will turn away from the faith, will betray and hate each other. Many false prophets will appear and deceive many people. Because of wickedness, the love of most will grow cold (Matthew 24:9-12).

3. Sign of the gospel is preached to the whole world. "The gospel will be preached in the whole world as a testimony to all nations, and then the end will come" (Matthew 24:14).

4. Sign of great distress in the world. "There will be great distress, unequaled from the beginning of the world until now – and never to be equaled again" (Matthew 24:21) -- A hint at Armageddon.

5. Sign of natural catastrophe of epic proportion. "Immediately after the distress of those days, the sun will be darkened, and the moon will not give its light; the

stars will fall from the sky, and the heavenly bodies will be shaken" (Matthew 24:29).

6.   Sign of the appearance of the Son of Man in the sky. "At that time the sign of the Son of Man will appear in the sky, and all the nations of the earth will mourn. They will see the Son of Man coming on the clouds of the sky, with power and great glory" (Matthew 24:30).

7.   Sign of the gathering of his elect from all corners of the earth [the rapture] (Matthew 24:31). "Two men will be at the field; one will be taken and the other left. Two women will be grinding a hand mill; one will be taken and the other left" (Matthew 24:40). A vivid description of the second coming of Christ wherein believers and the church will be lifted to the sky and escape tribulations.

PSYCHOLOGICAL IMPLICATIONS OF END-TIME PROPHESY

With the description and prediction of the terrible events at end time, it must have troubled Jesus's disciples, and by implications, will be for all believers. Yet, Jesus did not leave them hanging with anxiety and fears. He forewarned and reassured them, and urged them to be emotionally prepared in the following ways:

Lesson 1. Do not be alarmed. "You will hear of wars and rumors of wars, but see to it that you are not alarmed. Such things must happen, but the end is still to come" (Matthew 24:6). Forewarned is forearmed. Fulfillment of many Daniel's prophecies and foretelling the ones to come should prompt you to take biblical exhortations seriously. If the past is a good predictor of the future, as in Noah's days, you have a choice in believing the authenticity of biblical predictions or not. Regardless of your persuasion, the pace of the events of the world now appeared to have quickened since the founding of the Nation of Israel in 1948. The biblical prophecy of the re-gathering of Israel after two thousand years since her exile is a significant confirmation of God's continual unfolding of His plan for the ages. Christians believe we're still in the age of grace. God's grace and salvation in Christ is still open to all. As believer, you will note the above happenings, but should not be beset with anxiety or panic. Just as Jesus reassured his disciples--that they will not be abandoned when he was about to be led to his crucifixion and resurrection--you can be comforted by the refrain, "Let not your hearts be troubled" (John 14:1). Believers will not be abandoned but spared of the tribulations as they will be lifted to the sky during Christ's second coming.

Lesson 2. Stand firm on faith. "He who stand firm to the end will be saved" (Matthew 24:13). Clearly, as Daniel and his three friends had demonstrated, God will deliver those who stand firm on his or her faith. Armed with the knowledge that God is in control of human destiny, you too can have the confidence to endure, and not drift away in your faith as some are predicted to do.

Lesson 3. Be vigilant. "Therefore keep watch, because you do not know on what day your Lord will come" (Matthew 24:42). Vigilance will encourage you to prepare for the future and live a God-centered life to shun sins, shameful behaviors, and evil. In Noah's day, people ignored God's warning and went about doing their businesses. When the flood came, it was too late. Noah listened to the Lord. He was vigilant and took action. Consequently, he and his family were saved. You, too, if you listen and remain vigilant, would be saved, and enter into a fellowship with God through Christ.

In the Book of Revelation, Christ extended this invitation, "Those whom I love I rebuke and discipline. So be earnest, and repent. Here I am stand at the door and knock. If anyone hears my voice and opens the door, I will come in and eat with him, and he with me" (Revelation 3:19-20).

Lesson 4. Be prepared. "So you also must be ready, because the Son of Man will come at an hour when you least expect him" (Matthew 24:44). Anticipating the second coming of Christ is like living in San Francisco, an earthquake-prone area. You cannot predict when the next big earthquake will come, but you can prepare for it. In the same manner, Christ gave three parables on how you can be prepared for his second coming:

1. As the faithful and wise servant, whom the master has put in charge of the servants in his household, and faithfully discharging his/her duties by giving food at the proper time (Matthew 24:45).

2. As the five wise virgins who are prepared for Christ's coming by taking oil in jars along with their lamps while waiting for their bridegroom (Matthew 25:1-13).

3. As the good and faithful servants who were entrusted to invest their talents of money and faithfully and wisely using their talents (Matthew 25:14-25).

Anticipating the second coming of Christ at any day or time means that you have to reorder your priorities. You are urged to discharge your duties as faithful servants of Christ. Paul reminded us that, "We are God's workmanship, created in Christ to do good works, which God prepared us in advance to do" (Ephesians 2:10). Whether in caring for the household of God, utilizing your talents, or be spiritually prepared as the virgin waits for the coming of the bridegroom [Christ], you are expected to conduct yourselves as if Christ is coming at *any* moment unannounced. This attitude should pervade your daily living and spirituality.

Lesson 5. Do good deeds in the name of Christ. Christ told us to bless others through your actions--feed the hungry, quench those who are thirsty, invite the stranger into your household, clothe the needy, look after the sick, visit those in prison (Matthew 25:35-46). James, the brother of Jesus, reminded Christians, "Religion that God our Father accepts as pure and faultless is this: to look after orphans and widows in their distress and to keep oneself from being polluted by the world" (James 1:27). Doing good deeds and keeping yourselves holy are the hallmark of a vibrant Christian life. Your deeds, not your words, will be accounted for during judgment day. As the Son of Man comes and sits on the throne of glory, he will judge people by their deeds. He will separate the people as a shepherd separates the sheep from the goats--sheep to his right, goats to his left. Those on the right will be blessed because of their actions. The left will be cursed and thrown into eternal fire (Matthews 25:41). Daniel also affirmed this-- "multitudes who sleep in the dust of the earth will awake: some to everlasting life, others to shame and everlasting contempt" (Daniel 12:2). People will ask, "When did we see you (Christ) hungry or thirsty or a stranger or needing clothes or sick or in prison, and did not help you?" Christ's answer: "Whatever you did for one of the least of these brothers of mine, you did it for me" (Matthew 25:40). "Whatever you did not do for one of the least of these, you did not do for me" (Matthew 25:45).

In this context, Christ will judge you according to the authenticity of your faith manifested through actions. When you are able to translate your faith into actions to help your fellow human beings in the name of Christ, you do it for our Savior. This is the essence of Christian religion and psychospiritual empowerment, beliefs backed by action, through faith, hope, and love.

Chapter 22: KEY POINTS

1. The book of Daniel referenced many prophecies related to end-time events.

2. Both Daniel and Jesus used the phrase, "the abomination that causes desolation" to describe end-time events. Jesus's description of signs of the end time amplifies Daniel's end-time prophecy.

3. Believing what both Daniel and Jesus said about end time could empower you to be emotionally prepared.

CONCLUSION

This book analyzes Daniel's psychospirituality, and provides ten lessons, backed by research findings, from which you can apply to empower your life.

Amidst tribulations and uncertain time, Daniel, a man of God, stepped forward and stood firm on his faith. Daniel overcame the shame and humiliation of a defeated people. He worked his way to the highest position in the gentile kings' court. His faith was tested to the extreme degree. God used him to foretell the vision of the world to come. He became a beacon to his people during the dark night of Jewish Diaspora.

What made him so distinctive?

Daniel was a man who early in his youth chose God and remained steadfast in his faith. This trait and his early life's decision served him well throughout his career. God gave him and his friends wisdom and knowledge and delivered them from dangers. Daniel's attention to bodily and moral need as reflected in his careful choice of food, and his wise tact and diplomatic skills enabled him to live long, and to successfully navigate the dense political intrigues surrounding a man of high position and power in foreign courts. And Daniel led a prayerful life, always maintaining the spiritual lifeline between him and his Lord.

Daniel's unique character and life exemplified and testified to the following:

1. God can use an exceptional intellectual person to accomplish His will.

2. What a godly public servant is like.

3. What a true patriot would do to lead and inspire.

4. How psychospirituality can empower to transcend worldly conflicts.

5. How God uses dreams, visions and the connection to the unconscious to reveal His will.

6. How dream and visions are used in connecting prophecies of the Old and New Testament.

7. God is in control of human destiny.

8. There is Hope amidst despairs, life after death.

9. If you are willing to stand with God, God in turn will stand by you.

Psychospirituality is indispensable if you want to live fully your potentials. It needs to be cultivated and taken roots in your personality, and find expression in life. It can empower you. In the present materialistic world with a culture of unbelief, the life of Daniel, as during his time, reminds you that a steadfast faith in God can be a bulwark of strength and a source of inspiration to others. Daniel's life is a testament that you, too, can reach a deeper level of personality development that reaches out to enlighten and influence the world around you, like shining stars at night.

As in Daniel's day, we live in uncertain time. War, disasters, pestilence, and turmoil surround us and seemed to indicate that human history is moving inexorably towards the fulfillment of the end of time as Daniel had prophesied. Thinking about them is despairing and depressing. Yet, there is a gentle whisper amidst the fire.

As Christ stilled the storm at the Sea of Galilee, he can calm your anxiety. Christ reminds you to keep faith, be calmed and have hope in Him. God *is* in control of human history, of human environment, and of human lives. He still reaches out to you if you are ready to respond and commit to Him.

Thus, Daniel's behaviors and his psychospirituality challenge you--given your free will, how will you exercise it? Do you hear God's calling? Like Daniel, do you want to be psychospiritually empowered?

GLOSSARY

Apocalypse: A prophetic disclosure or revelation.[98]

Apocalyptic literature: "symbolic visionary prophetic literature, composed during oppressive conditions, consisting of visions whose events are recorded exactly as they were seen by the author and explained through a divine interpreter, and whose theological content is primarily eschatological."[99]

A'ram: A Son of Shem, progenitor of the Aramaean people (Gen 10:22-23), who spread widely in Syria and Mesopotamia from the Lebanese Mountains, to beyond the Euphrates and from the Taurus Range on the North to Damascus and northern Palestine on the South...During the long period of Israel's sojourn in Egypt, their wanderings in the Sinaitic Wilderness, and the extended period of the Judges in Canaan, the Aramaeans were multiplying and extending in every direction, particularly southward.[97] (92) *See* Arama'ic

Arama'ic: A Northwest Semitic dialect spoken by the Chaldeans of the book of Daniel (2:4-7:28). Since the Chaldeans are known to have generally spoken Akkad., Aramaic was inaccurately called Chaldee (Chadaic), a term that has been abandoned. "Aramaic became the lingua franca of all Southwest Asia as the result of the traffic of Aramaean merchants; business documents, weights, measures, etc., are found in Aram. dating in the eight to the fifth century B.C.

Jesus spoke Galilean Aramaic. The Greeks called Aram *Syria*; consequently, the language is called 'Syriac' (Daniel 2:4, KJV). This designation is now confined to the Aram. dialect spoken at Edessa, which became the language of the Christian churches of Syria and Mesopotamia. *See* Aram. [97] (92)

Armageddon: The battleground of the centuries, described in Revelation, to be fought on the ancient plain of Megiddo in Palestine, "in which the Lord, at His advent of glory, will deliver the Jewish remnant besieged by the Gentile world powers under the Beast (Revelation 13:1-10) and the false prophets (13:11-18)…. This last grand battle of the 'times of the Gentiles' and of this present age finds fulfillment in the striking stone prophecy of Daniel 2:35 and ushers in 'the day of the Lord' when God actively and visibly manifests His glorious power to the discomfiture and utter destruction of His enemies.[97] (103).

Dream: "Dream is a domain of experience, having an intellectual, ethical, and spiritual significance." The intellectual refers to the knowledge or thought that is conceived during sleep and is brought forward while awakened. The ethical aspect refers to one's true nature that manifests itself, without the "censorship" that occurs during the waking state. Spiritual significance suggests dreams as a mean of direct and communication of God with men. "The witness of conscience may make itself objective and expand within the dreamlike into perceptible transactions between God and man."[97] (pp. 317-318]. *See* Vision

Empowerment. A positive, dynamic process that focuses on one's strength, rights, and capabilities by which one gains control over one's affairs

Eschatology. The theological term to employed to designate the doctrine of the last things, particularly those dealing with the second coming of Christ, and the events preceding or following this great event. [97](373)

Locus of Control. A sense of inner control over stressful events and neuroticism.

Mindfulness. The awareness that emerges through paying attention on purpose, in the present moment, and non-judgmentally to things as they are.[100]

Neuroticism. Personality traits that produce chronic negative affectivity characterized by feeling anxious, tense, moody, or insecure that amplifies stressful responses in human.

Oneiromancy. Divination by Dream.[98] (p.918).

Prophecy. The oral or written message of a prophet...The genius of prophecy was rather a prediction of the future arising from the conditions of the present and was inseparably connected with the profoundly religious and spiritual message the prophet was called upon to proclaim to his own generation.[97] (pp. 1039-1040).

Prophecy is an emanation sent forth by God through the medium of the Active Intellect, first to man's rational faculty and then to his imaginative faculty. [101]

Psychospirituality. A blending of psychology and spirituality that connotes a strong religious sentiment (William James, M.D.), with an expansion of the bio-psycho-social model of health and disease (George Engel, M.D.) to include the spiritual dimension and that its applicability in clinical encounters.

Purpose in Life. A sense of overarching meaning (extending beyond a particular situation) effecting health outcomes via specific psychological mediators (e.g. changes in appraisal or coping mechanisms that produce negative affect.

Religion. The external, ritualistic practices of one's faith, "particular tradition, practice, or community that shapes a comprehensive world-view sufficient to interpret all of human experience within a specific cultural context." [115]

Resilience. The ability to recover quickly from illness, change, or misfortune.[98] (1106)

Spirituality. The inner core of one's religious beliefs and is attributed to the nearly human universal search for meanings, often involving some sense of transcendence.[115]

Telomere. DNA-protein complexes that cap chromosomal ends and promote chromosomal stability. They serve as a marker of biological age.

Telomerase. An enzyme that repairs chromosomal ends and forestalls telomere shortening. The stress hormone cortisol inhibits telomerase activity.

Vision: "A supernatural presentation of certain scenery or circumstances to the mind of a person while awake."[97] (1355). *See* Dream

Appendix

Research Issues in the Psycho-Spiritual Study of Daniel

Methodological Issues:

Although much has been written about the prophet Daniel, the study of the *Daniel, the man* is still fraught with methodological challenges. First, the Book of Daniel is a book of paradoxes. It is part history and part prophecies. It is originally written in two languages, Aramaic and Hebrew. Second, controversies exist regarding the dating of the book. Some of the accuracy of the historical events and even the authorship of the book have been questioned.[102] Some biblical scholars dated the book to the 6th century B.C.; others argued for a later date, around 2nd century B.C. Some accepted with certainty that Daniel, the man existed and that he is the author of the book that bears his name. Others thought different writers contributed to the writing of the book and that Daniel's name was chosen to portray their views and concerns, a form of writing called *pseudopigraphia* – writing under an assumed name.[103] Given these paradoxes and controversies, how should we approach the study of the character of Daniel?

Cornfeld has pointed out that the ancient writers of the scripture were less concerned with history than with theology.[104] Most ancient Jewish or Christian writers were careful to select materials that they regarded would preserve and advance their orthodoxy.[105] Thus, important historical materials may at times be omitted, and great lesson of spirituality, ethics and moral were emphasized. The Book of Daniel is no exception. So that when seen in this light, even though there may have been some discrepancies in recorded historical facts, the fact remains that the writer of the book of Daniel is keenly interested in portraying the human and divine aspects of events from a theological perspective. Rowley reminds us that, as a religious book, the value of Daniel as a spiritual text lies not in the accuracy of historical traditions, but rather in imparting a divine message[106]… "The book has something of man…and something of God in it."[107]

Since we are primarily interested in the psychological study of Daniel's character as portrayed by the writer, and the hermeneutic interpretation of its spiritual and moral lessons, it is in this context that we shall approach the study of Daniel. We are fortunate that a wealth of information about Daniel is portrayed in the book. We shall accept *ipso facto* what is written about Daniel is accurate and that Daniel is the writer who wrote the book that bears his name. And in the psycho-spiritual analysis of Daniel's character and his spirituality, we shall follow the chronology of the events in his book as the writer of Daniel had intended.

Conceptual Issues:

WHAT IS PSYCHOSPIRIŢUALITY?

Psychospirituality, as used in this volume, connotes three layers of meanings:

First, psychospirituality refers to William James's idea of *religious sentiment* that is highly motivating. It is that sentiment that motivated Mother Theresa to devote her entire life serving God by administering to the poor, downtrodden, neglected, and dying. The same sentiment sent Albert Schweitzer to travel deep into Lambarene, Gabon in Africa to serve in a hospital there. Used destructively, it causes a person to willingly blow oneself up much as terrorists do.

William James, MD, Harvard professor, the great American philosopher, and father of American psychology pointed out the powerful motivating effect of religion and religious sentiment. In his famous Gifford lecture on the *Varieties of Religious Experiences,* given at Scotland in 1902, James defined religion as follows:

> *"Religion, therefore ...shall mean for us the feelings, acts, and experiences of individual men in their solitude, so far as they apprehend themselves in relation to whatever they may consider the divine."* [108]

By "divine", James broadly defined it to mean "any object that is *godlike*, whether it be a concrete deity or not."[109] Being *godlike* has many qualities, among which are conceptions, ideas, or beliefs that are conceived to be the "first things in ways of being and power."[110] "They overarch and envelop, and from them there is no escape."[111] To James, religion is *"man's total reaction to life."*[112] It involves your total attitude towards existence as well. James argued that these systems of thoughts could stir in you strong sentiments called *religious sentiments* that are as real as any concretized experience that your sensory systems could evoke.[113] Thus, in James's view, when you consider something *godlike*, that entity is going to impel you to actions. In short, *religious sentiment* can empower because belief links to the "divine" is so compelling. The purpose of this volume is to recognize this sentiment and to direct it towards constructive ends. This book will attempt to show you how to harness psycho-spiritual power through Daniel's example to enhance your love, happiness, peace, wisdom, hope and resilience.

Second, psychospirituality connects the discipline of biology, psychology and religion and makes it holistic. As a way of looking at human behavior, psycho-spiritual approach adds a layer of spiritual understanding to the prevalent biological, psychological and socio-logical (bio-psycho-social [BPS]) conception of the human behav-ior[114] that operates in the context of culture.

Third, psychospirituality applies and extends the "clinical method" that a clinician or mental health practitioner uses in the analysis of the mental health states toward the understanding of spir-itual phenomenon. When applied to the study of current or histor-ical individuals, including biblical characters, it attempts to capture the totality of the person's experience; i.e., cognitive -- what the per-son said and thought (the recorded words); affective or emotion -- (tone of his speech, etc.); behavior -- (behavioral reaction to events) as well as the historical and cultural context in which the experience had occurred. Pulling together all these information, you can begin to understand the person's state of the mind and inner life and get a sense of his/her characteristic personality and behavioral pattern. To the extent a person's beliefs, convictions, testimonies, actions and values are related to the exercise of one's faith and to one's relation to the "divine", you then can infer from these data about that person's psychospirituality.

SPIRITUALITY DEFINED

Since the focus of this book is on connecting psychology (dis-cipline of studying and understanding human behavior) and spiri-tuality, what is meant by "spirituality"? There are many definitions of spirituality. Some authors differentiate spirituality from religion.

Religion usually refers to the external, ritualistic practices of your faith, "particular tradition, practice, or community that shapes a comprehensive world-view sufficient to interpret all of human experience within a specific cultural context."[115]. Spirituality, on the other hand, can be considered the inner core of your religious beliefs and is attributed to "the nearly human universal search for meanings, often involving some sense of transcendence."[116] Some would equate spirituality with "world-view."[117] The term "worldview", though used widely, seemed to imply a more cognitive emphasis. In contrast, psychospirituality emphasizes a more holistic and dynamic approach. This distinction is only artificial. For in reality, whether you consider yourself religious, spiritual or not, you practice what you believe. Consciously or unconsciously, you hold a "worldview" that guides your behavior. If you believe in prayer, for example, it exemplifies your belief in a power greater than yourself, and that through supplication you may obtain divine blessings. Authentic ritual of prayer is a reflection of your core belief. These two inter-related phenomena -- religion and spirituality; psychospirituality and worldview -- like yin-yang, couldn't be separated. In this volume, psychospirituality and worldview are used interchangeably.

THE MANIFESTATION OF PSYCHOSPIRITUALITY

How does psychospirituality manifest itself in your life? In the exercise of spirituality, the manifest phenomenon can either be sudden/dramatic or hidden/insidious. Saul's conversion to Christianity was dramatic. Saul was acting out of his deep "religious sentiment" as a devout Pharisee on the road to Damascus to arrest the Christians and bring them to persecution. His conversion was related in Acts 9:

> As he neared Damascus on his journey, suddenly a light from heaven flashed around him. He fell to the ground and heard a voice say to him, "Saul, Saul, why do you persecute me!"
> "Who are you, Lord?" Saul asked.
> "I am Jesus, whom you are persecuting," he replied. "Now get up and go into the city, and you will be told what you must do." (Acts 9:3-6)

This dramatic experience changes his life 180⁰. From being a persecutor of Christians, Saul (renamed Paul after his conversion) becomes Christianity's greatest advocate and missionary. On the other hand, the path of spiritual transformation of the apostle Peter and James, the brother of Jesus who later became early church leaders is insidious. Both Peter and James had had first-hand contact and experience witnessing the working of the power and miracles of Jesus. But both were initially skeptical of Jesus' claim of his divine identity. It took them quite a while to come to grip with the realization and acceptance that Jesus indeed is the Messiah, the Son of God. When that happened, they became totally changed individuals.

Since most people's spiritual transformation appears more insidious, you will be guided by the use of the more hidden and insidious manifestation of spiritual transformation in the study of Daniel's personality and spirituality. In this regard, you may consider the phenomenon of spirituality as follow.[118]

Spirituality manifests itself as a quieter, more gradual, and sometimes imperceptible transformation of the totality of your personality that is sustained over time.[119] The change affects all realms of your personality: cognition (thinking), emotion and behavior. It is an on-going process. That behavioral change is linked to a belief in a higher order, as in a belief in a god. Significant personal events such as a life-threatening accident, affliction with a serious illness, marriage, the birth of a child, separation and divorce, retirement or the death of loved ones all could induce and initiate this change. As a result, there is a gradual development and expression of a religious sentiment that defines more sharply the contour of your meaning and purpose in life. The positive transformation may be palpable. A sense of inner peace that surpasses understanding may ensure. A feeling of living in a state of *grace* may give you new confidence in moving through the routines of daily life. In such a state of mind, your perception of daily events may assume a different dimension: the rose smells sweeter, the day seems brighter, a smile becomes friendlier. You can walk down main street and encounter myriads of opportunity to do good as in simply saying "hello" to a homeless person or in sharing a dollar, or picking up a banana peel to prevent others from slipping and falling. There is a harmonious sense of unity of your ego with your ego-ideal as reflected in the desire to identify your character traits with the *character* of the one you defined as the "divine."

Difference Between Dream and Vision

Dreams occurred during sleep. Visions happened during conscious moment. "Vision is a supernatural presentation of certain scenery or circumstances to the mind of a person while awake."[120]

Although dream and vision are closely related, in classical prophecy, it appears that "dreams and visions are two distinct phenomenon, although visions can also take place at night." Dream is sometimes described as a "night vision", certain visions that are supposed to be seen during the night. Imageries in Daniel's dreams were described as "visions that passed though the mind" (Daniel 2:28, 4:5, 7:2).

Dream and vision differ in structure. "Dream accounts treat symbolic visions and words of prophecy separately and differently (hence the distinction between symbolic dream and message dream), the prophetic vision's genre combines what is seen and what is heard in the same narrative, that is the visual allegory, its interpretation and the message."[121] In visions, there is also a dialogue between the visionary and God (or an angel) and a word of prophecy.[122] In spite of the formal and stylistic difference between dreams and visions, their close relationship has encouraged critics to consider the prototype of vision as "dream + interpretation."[123]

During dreaming, strong emotions are aroused from deeper sub-cortical areas of the brain in both prophetic dreams and visions. In vision, the higher center of the brain, the cortical area, particularly the frontal lobe that subsumes logical, imaginative, associative and executive function of the human brain and mind, is much more fully engaged. Thus, the imageries and metaphors in visions are more straightforward, as contrasted with the manifest contents of dreams which may appear as "disguised" representations of underlying latent messages and require a seer to interpret them. Images conveyed through visions are visual although these may be accompanied by auditory phenomena.

As indicated in the Bible, God used visions at critical moments in human history to clearly reveal his will. In the New Testament, God used vision to convey to Peter and Paul his grand plan of salvation of the world, to include both Jews and gentiles. In Peter's case, the opening of the gospel to the gentile world was initially conveyed simultaneously in a vision to both Cornelius, a gentile Roman Centurion, and Peter, a Jew (Acts 10). God used vision to bring his servants together to clearly impart the message that the gospel of the salvation in Christ was for all people. Peter was commanded three times by a "voice" to "kill and eat impure animals" that God had "made clean" (Acts 10:15). God used vision to unequivocally instruct Peter and the early church to break out of the pre-conceived Jewish cultural tradition to open widely the door of salvation to all people, including gentiles, who were considered "impure".

In Paul's case, God used vision to divert his plan to preach the gospel in Bithynia, in Asia Minor, currently Northern Turkey and to go instead to Macedonia (Acts 16:6-9); thus bringing the gospel to European countries, and from there, eventually to Greece, Rome, and the whole world.

ABOUT THE AUTHOR

Albert C. Gaw, M.D. is a Clinical Professor of Psychiatry, University of California, San Francisco; a distinguished life fellow of the American Psychiatric Association (APA); and a past Speaker of the Assembly of the American Psychiatric Association.

An expert on cross-cultural psychiatry, Dr. Gaw currently is engaged in the study of psychospirituality of biblical characters and on brain mechanisms under spiritual conditions.

Among Dr. Gaw's numerous publications are four books: *Cross-Cultural Psychiatry*; *Culture, Ethnicity and Mental Illness*; *Concise Guide to Cross-Cultural Psychiatry*; and *The Eyes of the Heart: The Biblical Path to Spirituality and Inner Empowerment.*

Dr. Gaw's current research is on psycho-spirituality of biblical characters. The current volume, *Empowered*, focuses on how to harness psycho-spiritual resources to empower your life.

ENDNOTES

1   Rappaport J. Studies in empowerment: Introduction to the issue. In: Rappaport J, Swift C, Hess R (eds). *Studies in Empowerment: Steps to Understanding and Action.* New York: Haworth, 1984.

2   Robert KJ. Patient empowerment in the United States: a critical commentary. *Health Expectations.* 1999:2:82-92.

3   NIV Study notes 1:6-7,1320.

4   NIV Study notes 1:7.1320.

5   NIV Study notes 1:8,1320.

6   Macartney, Clarence Edward. *The Greatest Man of the Bible.* New York: Abingdon-Cokesbury Press, 1961, 190-191.

7   Ibid., 192.

8   Boantrophy connotes a mental illness in which the afflicted person acts like an animal. This is not a term familiar to most contemporary psychiatrists and mental health professionals.

9   American Psychiatric Association. *Diagnostic and Statistical Manual of Mental Disorders,* Fourth Edition. Washington, DC: American Psychiatric Association, 1994.

10   NIV Study note 7:4-7, 1330-1331.

11   Tremper, Longman III. *Daniel. The NIV Application Commentary.* Grand Rapids, Michigan: Zondervan, 1999, 189-190.

12   Archer, Jr., Gleason L. *A Survey of Old Testament:* Introduction. Chicago: Moody Press, 1964.

13   Darius the Medes. See NIV Study note 5:31, 1328.

14   NIV Study notes 9:24, 1334.

15   Walwoord, John F. *Daniel, The Key To Prophetic Revelation.* Chicago: Moody Press, 1989.

16   Mensch. A person having admirable characteristics, such as fortitude and firmness of purpose.

17   NIV Study notes 11:21,1338.

18   Phillips, John. *Exploring The Future.* Grand Rapids, Michigan: Kregel Publications, 2003, 59.

19   Ibid., 56.

20   Ibid,, 59.

21   NIV Study notes 9:25-27, 1335.

22   Jung, Carl G. *Man and His Symbols.* Garden City, New York: Double & Company Inc., 1964, 32.

23   Ibid., 82.

24 O'Donovan A, Tomiyama J, Lin J, Puterman E, Adler NE, Kemeny M, Wolkowitz OM, Blackburn EH, Epel ES. Stress appraisals and cellular aging: a key role for anticipatory threat in the relationship between psychological stress and telomere length. *Brain Behav Immun.* 2012 May; 26(4): 573-9. Epub 2012 Jan 24.

25 Husser, Jean-Marie. *Dreams and Dream Narratives in the Biblical World.* Sheffield, England: Sheffield Academic Press Ltd, 1999.

26 Ibid., 22.

27 Ibid.

28 Parker, Russ. *Dreams and Spirituality.* Bramcote, Nottingham NG9 3DS: Grove Books Limited, 1985.

29 Aserinsky E & Kleitman N. Regularly occurring periods of eye motility and concomitant phenomena during sleep. *Science,* 1953; 118: 273-274.

30 Dement W & Wolpert E. The relation of eye movements, body motility, and external stimuli to dream content. *Journal of Experimental Psychology,* 1958; 55(6): 543-553.

31 Kramer, Milton. *The Dream Experience: a Systematic Exploration.* New York: Routledge, 2007, 196.

32 Sohms M. *The Neuropsychology of Dreams: A Clinic-Anatomical Study.* Mahwah, NJ: Erlbaum, 1997.

33 Sohms M. Dreaming and REM sleep are controlled by different mechanisms. In E. Pace-Schot, E., Sohms, M., Blagrove, M. & Harnad, S. (eds.). *Sleep and Dreaming: Scientific Advances*

and Reconsiderations. Cambridge: Cambridge University Press, 2003, 51-58.

34   Fromm, Erich. *The Forgotten Language.* New York: Holt, Rinehart and Winston, 1962, 20.

35   Freud, Sigmund. *The Interpretation of Dreams.* New York: Avon Books, 1965.

36   Freud, Sigmund. *On Dreams.* New York: W. W. Norton & Company, Inc.,1952, 26.

37   Jung, Carl G. *Memories, Dreams, Reflections.* Aniela Jaffe (ed). New York: Vintage Books. 223.

38   Ibid., x.

39   Ibid., xi.

40   Yakovlev, Paul I. Motility, behavior and the brain. *J Nerv Mental Dis.* 1948; 107: 313-315.

41   Gaw, Albert C. *Concise Guide to Cross-Cultural Psychiatry.* Washington, DC: The American Psychiatric Publishing, Inc., 2001.

42   Sacks O and Hirsch J. A neurology of belief. Editorial. *Annals of Neurology.* February 2008; 63: 129-130. Doi: 10.1002/ana.21378.

43   Harris S, Sheth SA, Cohen MS. Functional Neuroimaging of belief, disbelief, and uncertainty. *Ann Neurol.* 2008; 63: 141-147.

44   Harris S, Kaplan JT, Curiel A, Bookheimer SY, Iacoboni M, et al. The Neural Correlates of Religious and Nonreligious

Belief. *PLoS ONE*. 2009; 4(10): e0007272. doi:10.1371/journal.pone.0007272

45   Ernst M, Pine DS, Hardin M. Triadic model of the neurobiology of motivated behavior in adolescence. *Psych Med*. Mar 2006; 36(3): 299-312.

46   Chester, Timothy. *The Message of Prayer*. Nottingham, England: InterVarsity Press, 2003.

47   Kleinman, Arthur. *Rethinking Psychiatry*. New York: Free Press, 1988.

48   O'Donovan A, Tomiyama J, Lin J, Puterman E, Adler NE, Kemeny M, Wolkowitz OM, Blackburn EH, Epel ES. Stress appraisals and cellular aging: a key role for anticipatory threat in the relationship between psychological stress and telomere length. *Brain Behav Immun*. May 2012; 26(4): 573-9. Epub 2012 Jan 24.

49   Dura-Vila G, Dein S, Littlewood R, and Leavey G. The Dark Night of the Soul: causes and resolution of emotional distress among contemplative nuns. *Transcultural Psychiatry*. 2010; 47: 548.

50   Frank, Jerome D. Psychotherapy, rhetoric and hermeneutics: implications for practice and research. *Psychotherapy*. 24: 293-302, 1987.

51   Edwards, Elizabeth. *Resilience*. New York: Broadway Books, 2009.

52   American Psychiatric Association. People Can Learn Markers On Road to Resilience. *Psychiatric News*. 19, 2007; 42(2): 5.

53   Koenig, Harold G. *Medicine, Religion, and Health*. West Conshohocken, PA: Templeton Foundation Press, 2008, 13.

54   Worthington EL, McCullough ME, & Sandage SJ. Empirical research on religion and psychotherapeutic processes and outcome: a 10-year review and research prospectus. *Psychological Bulletin*. 1996; 119: 448-487.

55   Koenig HG. (Editorial). Religion, spirituality and aging. *Aging & Mental Health*. January 2006; 10(1): 1-3.

56   Newberg A, Pourdehnad M, Alavi A, d'Aquili EG. Cerebral blood flow during meditative prayer: preliminary findings and methodological issues. *Percept Mod Skill*. October 2003; 972: 625-630.

57   Blackburn EH. Structure and function of telomeres. *Nature*. April 1991; 350: 569-573 | doi:10.

58   Choi J, Fauce SR, Effros RB. Reduced telomerase activity in T lymphocytes exposed to cortisol. *Brain, Behavior, and Immunity*. 2008; 22: 600-605.

59   Epel ES, Blackburn EH, Lin J, Dhabhar FS, Adler NE, Morrow JD, and Richard M. Cawthon RM. Accelerated telomere shortening in response to life stress. *PNAS*. December 2004; 101(49): 17312-17315.

60   Cawthon R, et al. Association between telomere length in blood and mortality in people aged 60 years or older. *Lancet*. 2003; 361: 393-395.

61   Wolkowitz OM, Mellon SH, Epel ES, Lin J, Reus VI, Rosser R, Burke H, Compagnone M, Nelson JC, Dhabhar FS and EH Blackburn EH. Resting leukocyte telomerase activity is

elevated in major depression and predicts treatment response. *Molecular Psychiatry.* 2011: 1-9.

62   Okereke OI, Prescott J, Jason Y. Y. Wong JYY, Han J, Kathryn M. Rexrode KM, De Vivo I. High phobic anxiety is related to lower leukocyte telomere length in women. *PLoS One.* July 2012; 7(7): e40516.

63   Epel ES, et al. The rate of leukocyte telomere shortening predicts mortality from cardiovascular disease in elderly men. *Aging.* January 2009; 1(1): 81-88.

64   Hoen PW, de Jonge P, Na BY, Farzaneh-Far R, Epel E, Lin J, Blackburn E, Whooley MA. Depression and leukocyte telomere length in patients with coronary heart disease: data from the Heart and Soul Study. *Psychosom Med.* September 2011; 73(7): 541-7.

65   Kume K, Kikukawa M, Hanyu H, Takata Y, Umahara T, Sakurai H, Kanetaka H, Ohyashiki K, Ohyashiki JH and Iwamoto T. Telomere length shortening in patients with dementia with Lewy bodies. *European Journal of Neurology.* 2012; 19: 905-910.

66   Farzaneh-Far R, Lin J, Epel E, Lapham K, Blackburn E, Whooley MA. Telomere length trajectory and its determinants in persons with coronary artery disease: Longitudinal findings from the Heart and Soul study. *PLoS One.* January 2010; 5(1): e8612.

67   Gardner JP, et al. Rise in insulin resistance is associated with escalated telomere attrition. *Circulation.* 2005; 111: 2171-2177.

68   O'Donovan A, Lin J, Dhabhar FS, Wolkowitz O, Tillie JM, Blackburn EH, and Epel E. Pessimism correlates with

leukocyte telomere shortness and elevated interleukin-6 in post-menopausal women. *Brain, Behavior Immun.* May 2009; 23(4): 446-449.

69   Kiefer A, Lin J, Blackburn, E, and Epel E. Dietary restraint and telomere length in pre- and post-menopausal women. *Psychosom Med.* October 2008; 70(8): 845-849.

70   Humphreys J, Epel ES, Cooper BA, Lin J, Blackburn EH and Lee KA. Telomere shortening in formerly abused and never abused women. *Biol Res Nurs.* 8 March 2011 DOI: 10.1177/1099800411398479.

71   O'Donovan A, Epel E, Lin J, Wolkowitz O, Cohen B, Maguen S, Metzler T, Lenoci M, Blackburn E, and Neylan TC. Childhood trauma associated with short leukocyte telomere length in posttraumatic stress disorder. *Biol Psychiatry.* 2011; 70: 465-471.

72   Entringer S, Epel ES, Kumsta R, Lin J, Hellhammer DH, Blackburn EH, Wüst S, and Wadhwa PD. Stress exposure in intrauterine life is associated with shorter telomere length in young adulthood. *PNAS.* August 2011; 108(33): ES13-E518.

73   Prather AA, Puterman E, Lin J, O'Donovan A, Krauss J, Tomiyama AJ, Epel ES, and Blackburn EH. Shorter leukocyte telomere length in midlife women with poor sleep quality. *J Aging Research.*2011: 721390.

74   Krauss J, Farzaneh-Far R, Puterman E, Na B, Lin J, Epel E, Blackburn E, Whooley MA. Physical fitness and telomere length in patients with coronary heart disease: findings from the Heart and Soul Study. *PLoS ONE.* November 2011; 6(11): e26983

75   Tomiyama AJ, O'Donovan A, Lin J, Puterman E, Lazaro A, et al. Does cellular aging relate to patterns of allostasis? An examination of basal and stress reactive HPA axis activity and telomere length. *Physiology & Behavior.* 2012; 106: 40-45.

76   Blackburn EH & Epel ES. Telomeres and adversity: too toxic to ignore. *Nature.* October 2012; 490:169-171.

77   O'Donovan A, Pantell MS, Puterman E, Dhabhar FS, et al. Cumulative inflammatory load is associated with short leukocyte telomere length in the Health, Aging and Body composition Study. *PLoS ONE.* May 2011; 6(5): e19687.

78   Wolkowitz OM, Mellon SH, Epel ES, Lin J, Dhabhar FS, Su Y, Reus VI, Rosser R, Burke HM, Kupferman E, Compagnone M, Nelson JC, Blackburn EH. Leukocyte telomere length in major depression: correlations with chronicity, inflammation and oxidative stress – preliminary findings. *PLoS One.* March 2011; 6(3): e17837.

79   Ludlow AT, Zimmerman JB, Witkowski S, Hearn JW, Hatfield BD, And Roth SM. Relationship between physical activity level, telomere length, and telomerase activity. *Med Sci Sports Exerc.* October 2008; 40(10): 1764-1771.

80   Puterman E, Lin J, Blackburn E, O'Donovan A, Adler N, et al. The power of exercise: buffering the effect of chronic stress on telomere length. *PLoS.* May 2010; 5(5): e10837.

81   Farzaneh-Far R, Lin J, Epel ES, Harris WS, Blackburn EH, Whooley MA. Association of marine omega-3 fatty acid levels with telomeric aging in patients with coronary heart disease. *JAMA.* 2010; 303(3): 250-257.

82   Lin J, Kroenke CH, Epel E, Kenna HA, Wolkowitz OM, Blackburn E, Rasgon NL. Greater endogenous estrogen expo-

sure is associated with longer telomeres in postmenopausal women at risk for cognitive decline. *Brain Research.* 2011: 224-231.

83   Hovatta L, de Mello VDF, Kananen L, Jaana Lindstrom J, et al. Leukocyte telomere length in the Finnish Diabetes Prevention Study. *PLoS.* April 2012; 7(4): e34948.

84   Ornish D, Lin J, Daubenmier J, Weidner G, Epel E, Kemp C, Magbanua MJM, Marlin R, Yglecias L, Carroll PR, Blackburn EH. Increased telomerase activity and comprehensive lifestyle changes: a pilot study. *Lancet Oncol.* 2008; 9:1048-57.

85   Jacobs TL, Epel ES, Lin J, Elizabeth H. Blackburn EH, Owen M. Wolkowitz OM, et al. Intensive meditation training, immune cell telomerase activity, and psychological mediators. *Psychoneuroimmunology.* June 2011; 26(5): 664-681.

86   Epel E, Daubenmier J, Judith T. Moskowitz JT, Susan Folkman S, and Blackburn, E. Can Meditation slow rate of cellular aging? Cognitive stress, mindfulness, and telomeres. *Ann N.Y. Acad Sci.* August 2009; 1172: 34-53.

87   Williams DR & Sternthal MJ. Spirituality, religion and health: evidence and research directions. *Med J Aust.* 2007; 186 (10): 47

88   Kabat-Zinn J. *Full Catastrophe Living.* New York: Delta Publishing, 1990.

89   Carmody J, Baer RA, Lykins E, Olendzki N. An empirical study of the mechanisms of mindfulness in a mindfulness-based stress reduction program. *J Clin Psychol.* Jun 2009; 65(6): 613-26.

90   Geary C and Rosenthal SL. Sustained Impact of MBSR on Stress, Well-Being, and Daily Spiritual Experiences for 1 Year in Academic Health Care Employees. *The Journal of Alternative and Complementary Medicine*. 2011; 17(10): 939–944. doi: 10.1089/acm.2010.0335.

91   Bower JE, et al. Benefit finding and physical health: positive psychological changes and enhanced allostasis. *Soc. Personal Psychol Compass*. 2008; 2: 223-244.

92   Fredrickson BL, et al. Open hearts build lives: Positive emotions, induced through loving-kindness meditation, build consequential personal resources. *Journal of Personality and Social Psychology*. Nov 2008; 95(5): 1045-1062. doi: 10.1037/a0013262

93   Aschbacher K, Epel E, Wolkowitz OM, Prather AA, Puterman E, Dhabhar FS. Maintenance of a positive outlook during acute stress protects against pro-inflammatory reactivity and future depressive symptoms. *Brain, Behavior, and Immunity*. 2012; 26: 346–352.

94   Litt MD. Cognitive mediators of stressful experience: self-efficacy and perceived control. *Cogn. Ther. Res.* 1988; 12(3): 241-260.

95   Shurgot GR, Knight BG. Influence of neuroticism, ethnicity, familism, and social support on perceived burden in dementia caregivers: pilot test of the transactional stress and social support model. *J Gerontol B Psychol Sci Soc Sci.* 2005 Nov; 60(6): P331-P334.

96   Holzel BK, Carmody J, Vangel M, Christina C, Yerramsetti SM, Gard T, Lazar SW. Mindfulness practice leads to increases in regional brain gray matter density. *Psychiatry Research: Neuroimaging*. 2011; 191: 36-43.

97   Unger, Merrill. *The New Unger Dictionary*. Chicago: Moody Press, 1988.

98   *The American Heritage Dictionary of the English Language. New College Edition,* Morris, W. (ed). Boston: Houghton Mifflin Co., 1976.

99   Alexander, Ralph. Abstract of *"Hermeneutics of Old Testament Apocalyptic Literature,"* Doctoral Dissertation).1.

100   Williams M, Teasdale J, Degal Z, and Kabat-Zinn J. *The Mindful Way Through Depression*. New York: The Guilford Press, 2007, 47.

101   [Attributed to Maimonides]. Guillame, Alfred. *Prophecy and Divination Among the Hebrews and Other Semites*. New York, NY: Harper and Brothers Publishers, 1938. 186.

102   Porteus, Norman. *Daniel: A Commentary.* Philadelphia: Westminster, 1965.

103   Cornfeld, Gaalyahu (ed). *Daniel to Paul.* New York, NY: Macmillan Company, 1962, 72.

104   Ibid.

105   Ibid.

106   Ibid.

107   Ibid., 180.

108   James, William. *The Varieties of Religious Experience*. New Hyde Park, New York: University Books, 1963, 29. (original edition 1902).

109   Ibid.,34.

110   Ibid.

111   Ibid.

112   Ibid.,35.

113   Ibid.

114   Engel, George L. *The need for a new medical model: A challenge for biomedicine. Science.* 1970; 196: 129–136.

115   Hall, DE, Kroenig HG, Meadow KG. "Conceptualizing 'religion": how language shapes and constrains knowledge in the study of religion and health" *Perspect Biol Med.* 2004; 47: 386-401.

116   Ibid.

117   Nicholi, Jr, Armand M. Introduction: Definition and Significance of a Worldview, in *Handbook of Spirituality and Worldview in Clinical Practice.* Josephson, Allan M. and Peteet, John (eds). Washington, DC: The American Psychiatric Publishing, Inc., 2004, 3-12.

118   Gaw, Albert C. *The Eyes of the Heart. The Biblical Path to Spirituality and Inner Empowerment.* Longwood, Florida: The Xulon Press, 2008, 23-29.

119   Ibid,, 26.

120   *The New Unger's Bible Dictionary.* Harrison, R. K. (Ed). Chicago: Moody Press, 1988.

121 Husser, Jean-Marie. *Dreams and Dream Narratives in the Biblical World*, Translated by Jill M Munro. Sheffield, England: Sheffield Academic Press, Ltd, 1999, 145-146.

122 Ibid., 145.

123 Ibid., 146.

www.ingramcontent.com/pod-product-compliance
Lightning Source LLC
Chambersburg PA
CBHW051138120626
46547CB00012B/856